Marie Barber's 515 Inspirational Cross-Stitch Designs

Sterling Publishing Co., Inc. New York
A Sterling/Chapelle Book

Chapelle

Owner
Jo Packham

Editor
Karmen Quinney

Staff
Ann Bear, Areta Bingham,
Kass Burchett, Rebecca Christensen,
Holly Fuller, Marilyn Goff,
Holly Hollingsworth, Shawn Hsu,
Susan Jorgensen, Pauline Locke,
Barbara Milburn, Linda Orton,
Leslie Ridenour, Cindy Stoeckl

Photography
Kevin Dilley/Hazen Photography

Photostylist
Jo Packham

 We would like to offer our sincere appreciation for the valuable support given in this ever changing industry of new ideas, concepts, designs, and products. Several projects shown in this publication were created with outstanding and innovative products developed by DMC Floss, Kreinik, Mill Hill Beads, Wichelt Fabric, and Zweigart Fabric.

Library of Congress Cataloging-in-Publication Data

Barber, Marie.
    Marie Barber's 515 inspirational cross stitch designs / Marie Barber.
        p.   cm.
    "A Sterling/Chapelle book."
    Includes index.
    ISBN 0-8069-6255-0
    1.Cross-stitch —Patterns.   2. Christian art and symbolism.
I. Title.   II. Title: 515 inspirational cross stitch designs.
III. Title: Five hundred fifteen inspirational cross stitch designs.
TT778.C76B383   1999   98–46796
746.44'3041—dc21   CIP
10 9 8 7 6 5 4 3 2 1

Published by Sterling Publishing Company, Inc.,
387 Park Avenue South, New York, NY 10016
© 1999 by Chapelle Limited
Distributed in Canada by Sterling Publishing
℅ Canadian Manda Group, One Atlantic Avenue, Suite 105
Toronto, Ontario, Canada M6K 3E7
Distributed in Great Britain and Europe by Cassell PLC
Wellington House, 125 Strand, London WC2R 0BB, England
Distributed in Australia by Capricorn Link (Australia) Pty Ltd.
P.O. Box 6651, Baulkham Hills, Business Centre, NSW 2153, Australia
Printed in the United States
All Rights Reserved

Sterling ISBN 0-8069-6255-0

If you have any questions or comments, please contact: Chapelle Ltd., Inc., P.O. Box 9252 Ogden, UT 84409 (801) 621-2777 • FAX (801) 621-2788 • E-mail Chapelle1@ aol.com

Marie Barber, born and raised in Kristianstad, Sweden, now lives in Ragland, Alabama, on the Coosa River with her husband and their two children.

Marie says she has always loved to draw and illustrate. At the age of 14, she was the youngest student to study oil painting under the instruction of the late Dr. Göran Trönnberg.

She came to the United States in 1983 as an exchange student, and in 1987, returned after being accepted to the Art Institute of Atlanta. She has freelanced as a novel illustrator for a Swedish weekly publication and her artwork is featured at Loretta Goodwin's Gallery in Birmingham, Alabama. Although she has explored several avenues of the art world, Marie says she found her passion in 1993 when she began designing cross-stitch patterns.

Table of Contents

Open your eyes that you may see
the wonder that around you lies;
it will enrich your every day
and make you glad and kind and wise.

ABCDEFGHIJKLMN
OPQRSTUVWXYZ

ABCDEFGHIJKLMNOPQRSTUVWXYZ
2 3 4 5 6 7 8 9 0

General Instructions

Introduction

Contained in this book are 515 counted cross-stitch designs.

Each page of graphed designs has its own color code. To create one-of-a-kind motifs, vary colors in graphed designs.

Fabric for Cross-stitch

Counted cross-stitch is worked on even-weave fabrics. These fabrics are manufactured specifically for counted-thread embroidery, and are woven with the same number of vertical as horizontal threads per inch.

Because the number of threads in the fabric is equal in each direction, each stitch will be the same size. The number of threads per inch in even-weave fabrics determines the size of a finished design.

Number of Strands

The number of strands used per stitch varies, depending on the fabric used. Generally, the rule to follow for cross-stitching is three strands on Aida 11, two strands on Aida 14, one or two strands on Aida 18 (depending on desired thickness of stitches), and one strand on Hardanger 22.

For backstitching, use one strand on all fabrics. When completing a french knot, use two strands and one wrap on all fabrics, unless otherwise directed.

Finished Design Size

To determine size of finished design, divide stitch count by number of threads per inch of fabric. When design is stitched over two threads, divide stitch count by half the threads per inch. For example, if a design with a stitch count of 120 width and 250 length were stitched on a 28 count linen over two threads, the end size would be 8⅝" x 17⅞".

Preparing Fabric

Cut fabric at least 3" larger on all sides than finished design size to ensure enough space for desired assembly.

To prevent fraying, whipstitch or machine-zigzag along raw edges or apply liquid fray preventive.

Needles for Cross-stitch

Blunt needles should slip easily through fabric holes without piercing fabric threads. For fabric with 11 or fewer threads per inch, use a tapestry needle size 24; for 14 threads per inch, use a tapestry needle size 24 or 26; for 18 or more threads per inch, use a tapestry needle size 26. Never leave needle in design area of fabric. It may leave rust or a permanent impression on fabric.

Floss

All numbers and color names on the codes represent the DMC brand of floss. Use 18" lengths of floss. For best coverage, separate strands and dampen with a wet sponge. Then put together the number of strands required for fabric used.

Centering the Design

Fold the fabric in half horizontally, then vertically. Place a pin in the fold point to mark the center. Locate the center of the design on the graph. To help in centering the designs, arrows are provided at left-side center and bottom center. Begin stitching all designs at the center point of graph and fabric.

Securing the Floss

Insert needle up from the underside of the fabric at starting point. Hold 1" of thread behind the fabric and stitch over it, securing with the first few stitches. To finish thread, run under four or more stitches on the back of the design. Never knot floss, unless working on clothing.

Another method of securing floss is the waste knot. Knot floss and insert needle down from the right top side of the fabric about 1" from design area. Work several stitches over the thread to secure. Cut off the knot later.

Carrying Floss

To carry floss, weave floss under the previously worked stitches on the back. Do not carry thread across any fabric that is not or will not be stitched. Loose threads, especially dark ones, will show through the fabric.

Cleaning the Finished Design

When stitching is finished, soak fabric in cold water with a mild soap for five to ten minutes. Rinse well and roll in a towel to remove excess water. Do not wring. Place work face down on a dry towel and iron on warm setting until the fabric is dry.

Cross-stitch (X st)

Stitches are done in a row or, if necessary, one at a time in an area.

1. Insert needle up between woven threads at A.

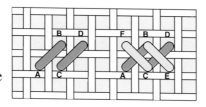

2. Go down at B, the opening diagonally across from A.

3. Come up at C and down at D, etc.

4. To complete the top stitches creating an "X", come up at E and go down at B, come up at C and go down at F, etc. All top stitches should lie in the same direction.

Backstitch (BS)

1. Insert needle up between woven threads at A.

2. Go down at B, one opening to the right.

3. Come up at C.

4. Go down at A, one opening to the right.

French Knot (FK)

1. Insert needle up between woven threads at A, using one strand of embroidery floss.

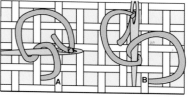

2. Loosely wrap floss once around needle.

3. Go down at B, the opening across from A. Pull floss taut as needle is pushed down through fabric.

4. Carry floss across back of work between knots.

Lazy Daisy Stitch (LD)

1. Insert needle up between woven threads at A.

2. Go down at B, using same opening as A.

3. Come up at C, crossing under two threads. Pull through, holding floss under needle to form loop.

4. Go down at D, crossing one thread.

Long Stitch (LS)

1. Insert needle up between woven threads at A.

2. Go down at B, crossing two threads. Pull flat.

Repeat A–B for each stitch. Stitch may be horizontal, verticle, or diagonal as indicated in examples 1, 2, and 3. The length of the stitch should be the same as the length indicated on the graph.

Satin Stitch (SS)

1. Insert needle up between woven threads at A.

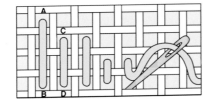

2. Go down at B, forming a straight stitch.

3. Come up at C and go down at D, forming another smooth straight stitch that is slightly overlapping the first.

4. Repeat to fill design area.

Bead Attachment (Bds), Crystal Treasure (CT), and Glass Treasure (GT)

Beads and treasures should sit facing the same direction as the top cross-stitch.

1. Make first half of a cross-stitch.

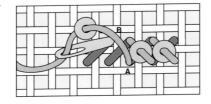

2. Insert needle up between woven threads at A.

3. Thread one bead before going down at B, the opening diagonally across from A.

4. To strengthen stitch, come up again at A and either go through bead again or split threads to lay around bead and go down at B again.

Working with Different Cross-stitch Elements

Depending on the type of elements used to create a cross-stitch piece, the same cross-stitch design can have several different looks. Use silk floss, overdyed floss, metallic thread, and beads to add dimension and texture to your projects.

The photo on the facing page features the same cross-stitch design that has been completed with four different elements: floss, overdyed floss, silk floss, and beads. The wreath graph and four codes representing the different elements can be found on page 10. *Note: The different codes have been provided for the wreath only. However, the different elements can be applied on any cross-stitch piece. Kreinik Conversion Chart can be found on pages 126-127.*

Silk Thread Tips

- Strands should be 12–15" in length.

- Color variation between skeins and bleeding of thread onto fabrics is common with silk thread.

- Silk thread can be combined with cotton thread in the same piece.

- When using variegated strands, cross each stitch as it is made rather than crossing the stitch on the way back across a row.

- Silk cross-stitched pieces should be dry-cleaned rather than hand-washed.

Thread Descriptions

Embroidery Floss is a stranded cotton and the most versatile thread available. **Overdyed Floss** is Egyptian cotton, overdyed by hand, creating a subtle shaded effect. **Rachel** ribbon is a tubular, nylon thread with a shimmery look. **Waterlillies** floss is a 12-ply hand-dyed silk with a subtle sheen look.

The threads listed above are distributed by **Anchor**, 30 Patewood Drive, Greenville, SC 29615; **DMC Corporation**, 10 Port Kearny, South Kearny, NJ 07032; **Kreinik Manufacturing Company Inc.**, 3106 Timanus Lane, Suite #101, Baltimore, MD 21244; **Needle Necessities, Inc.**, 14746 N.E. 95 St., Redmond, WA 98052; **The Caron Collection**, 67 Poland St., Bridgeport, CT 06605.

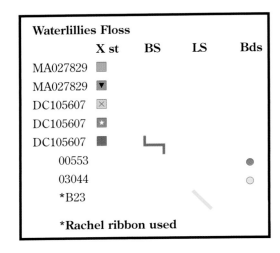

DMC Floss

	X st	BS	LS	Bds
472	■			
471	▼			
3348	⊠			
3347	✦			
3346	■	⌐		
00553				●
03044				○
*B23				╱

*Rachel ribbon used

Waterlillies Floss

	X st	BS	LS	Bds
MA027829	■			
MA027829	▼			
DC105607	⊠			
DC105607	✦			
DC105607	■	⌐		
00553				●
03044				○
*B23				╱

*Rachel ribbon used

Kreinik Silk Floss

	X st	BS	LS	Bds
2112	■			
2114	▼			
2121	⊠			
2123	✦			
2124	■	⌐		
00553	☐			●
03044	☐			○
*B23	☐			╱

*Rachel ribbon used

Mill Hill Beads

	Bds	LS
00525	■	
00167	▼	
00341	⊠	
02020	✦	
00332	■	
00553	●	
03044	○	
*B23		╱

*Rachel ribbon used

Stitch Count: 36 x 42

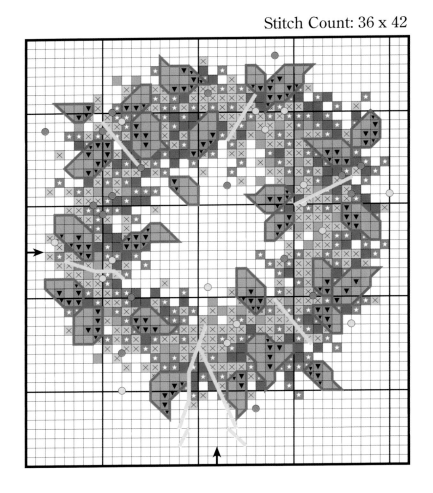

To Be Friends

Stitch Count: 40 x 21

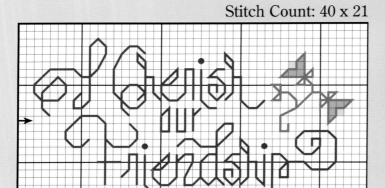

Stitch Count: 32 x 17

Stitch Count: 50 x 38

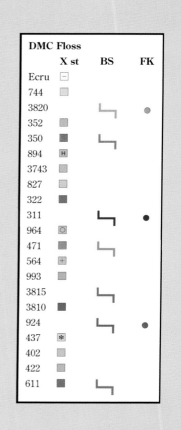

DMC Floss			
	X st	**BS**	**FK**
Ecru	–		
744			
3820		⌐	●
352			
350		⌐	
894	H		
3743			
827			
322			
311		⌐	●
964	◎		
471		⌐	
564	+		
993			
3815		⌐	
3810			
924		⌐	●
437	✳		
402			
422			
611		⌐	

Stitch Count: 17 x 23

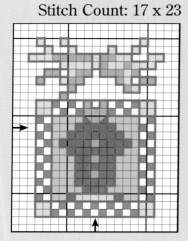

Stitch Count: 20 x 23

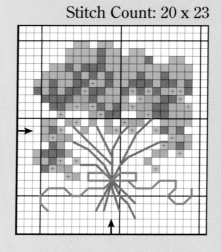

Stitch Count: 26 x 29

Stitch Count: 30 x 49

Stitch Count: 16 x 18

Stitch Count: 17 x 17

Stitch Count: 10 x 18

Stitch Count: 19 x 10
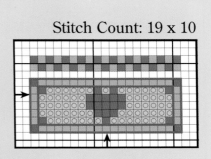

Stitch Count: 19 x 38
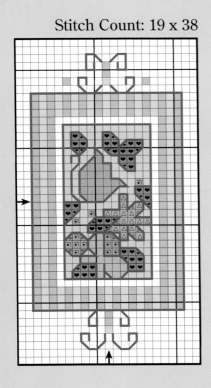

Stitch Count: 8 x 48
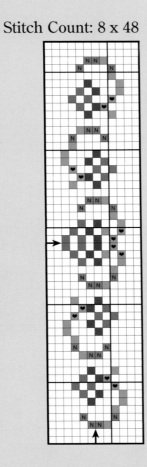

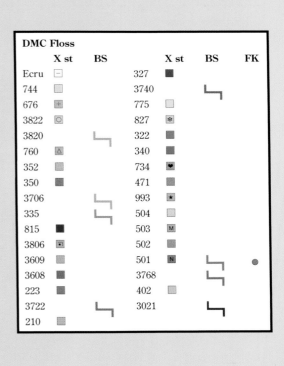

DMC Floss						
	X st	BS		X st	BS	FK
Ecru	⊟		327	■		
744			3740		⌐	
676	+		775			
3822	◎		827	✳		
3820		⌐	322	■		
760	△		340	■		
352			734	♥		
350	■		471	■		
3706		⌐	993	★		
335		⌐	504			
815	■		503	M		
3806	▪		502	■		
3609			501	N	⌐	●
3608	■		3768		⌐	
223	■		402		⌐	
3722		⌐	3021		⌐	
210						

Stitch Count: 40 x 55   Stitch Count: 29 x 30

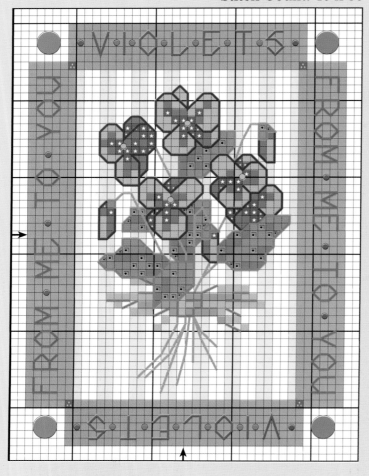

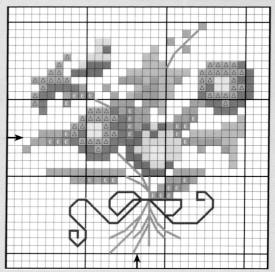

Stitch Count: 31 x 20

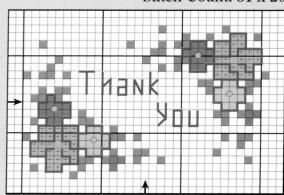

Stitch Count: 80 x 24

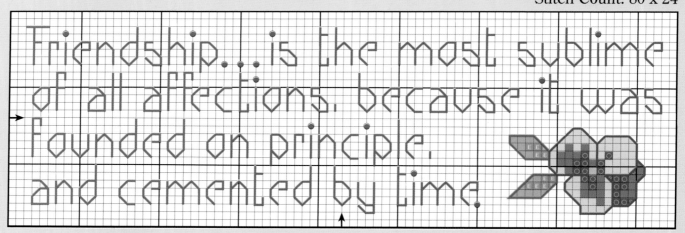

DMC Floss

	X st	FK		X st	BS		X st	BS	FK		X st	BS	FK		X st	BS	CT
712			3354			3747				472				924			
676		●	223			340				471				613			
729			3803			3807				989				420			
761			210			792			●	320				12209			
760			550			791				501			●				●

14

Stitch Count: 26 x 29

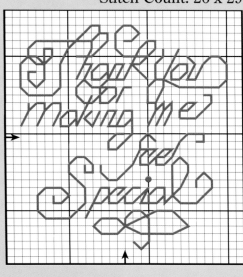

Stitch Count: 47 x 18

Stitch Count: 46 x 8

Stitch Count: 50 x 33

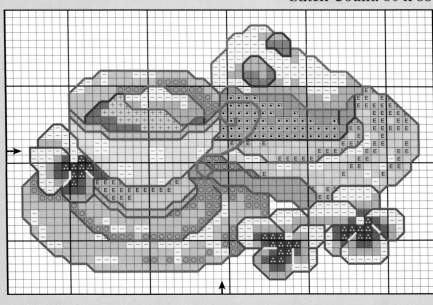

Stitch Count: 22 x 36

Stitch Count: 15 x 23

DMC Floss									
	X st	BS	FK		X st	BS	FK		X st	BS	FK
Ecru	□		○	3803			●	3815		
744				815				924		
3822				3743				3364		
3820	★			775				3363		
676				827	E			402		
729				341				437	+	
945				340				436	M	
352				322				435		
350			●	793				801		
3689				792				644		
3806				504				611		●
3608				503				3021		

Stitch Count: 28 x 48

Stitch Count: 9 x 26

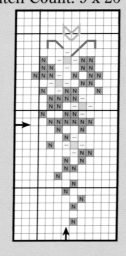

Stitch Count: 21 x 11

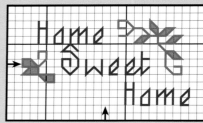

Stitch Count: 25 x 14

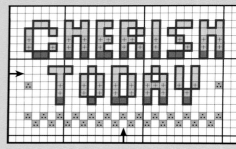

Stitch Count: 11 x 11

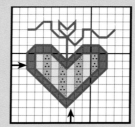

Stitch Count: 21 x 25

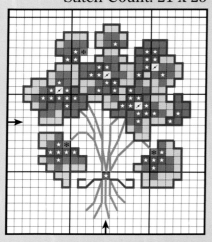

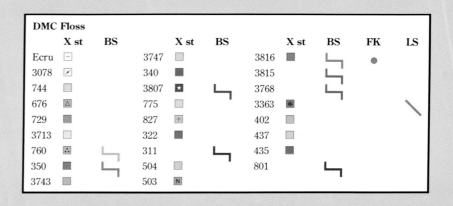

DMC Floss											
	X st	BS		X st	BS		X st	BS	FK	LS
Ecru	⊟		3747			3816		⌐	●	
3078	✦		340			3815		⌐		
744			3807	✦	⌐	3768		⌐		
676	△		775			3363	✦			╲
729			827	+		402				
3713			322			437				
760	✦	⌐	311		⌐	435				
350		⌐	504			801		⌐		
3743			503	N						

Stitch Count: 62 x 8

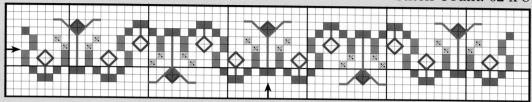

Stitch Count: 37 x 52

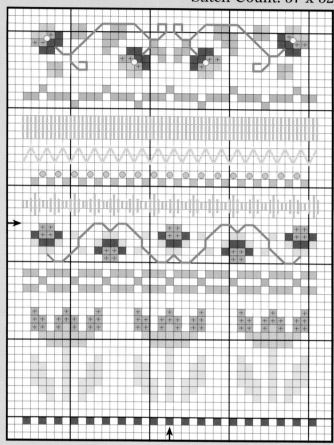

DMC Floss						
	X st	**BS**	**FK**	**LS**	**SS**	**Bds**
760						
776						
894						
893						
309						
3722						
3687						
3685						
3755						
772						
3348						
3347						
3346						
3363						
996						
3817						
3816						
3815						
924						
00123						
02003						
*MA115823						
*Overdyed floss used						

Stitch Count: 24 x 23

Stitch Count: 32 x 28

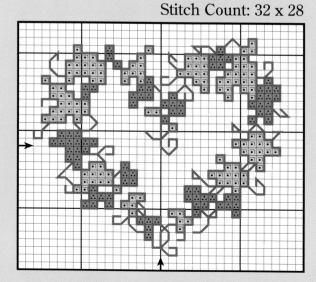

Stitch Count: 28 x 14

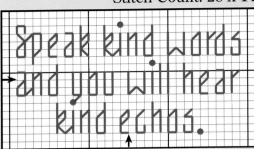

Stitch Count: 38 x 39

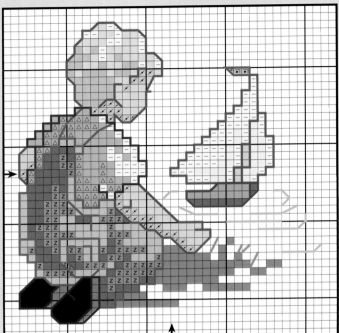

Stitch Count: 23 x 23

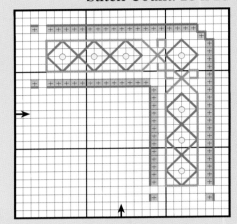

Stitch Count: 16 x 26

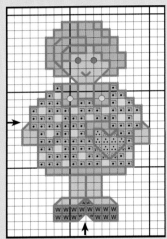

DMC Floss

	X st	BS	FK		X st	BS		X st	BS	FK	Bds
Ecru				3325			436				
727			○	932			422				
676	+			959			612	W			
3821				3813			611			●	
3045				502	z		3781				
951				3768			844				
945				924			3022				
760				471			3787				
351				739			3021	❋			
349				437	H		00123				○
221			●								

Stitch Count: 16 x 16

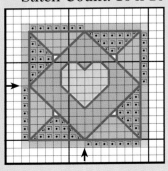

Stitch Count: 53 x 21

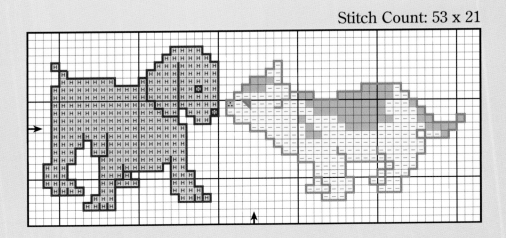

18

Stitch Count: 32 x 45

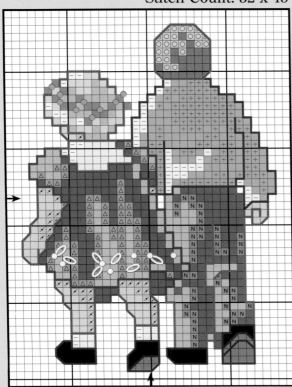

Stitch Count: 27 x 28

Stitch Count: 45 x 5

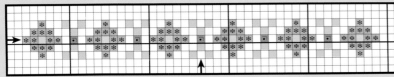

Stitch Count: 22 x 58

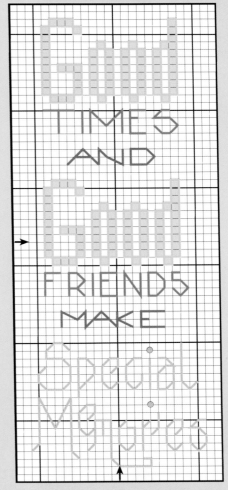

DMC Floss

	X st	BS	FK	LD		X st	BS	FK
Ecru	–		○	⬭	471	◼		
727					3363		⌐	
3821					3813			
951					502	N		
945					958		⌐	
760	✳				3810		⌐	
893		⌐	●		3768	◼		
352					924		⌐	
351	△		●		739	☐		
349	◼				436	◎	⌐	
221		⌐			435	◼		
3743					356		⌐	●
3041		⌐			3022	◼		
341	▪				3787	◼		
3325					3781		⌐	
932	+				844		⌐	
3348								

Stitch Count: 45 x 14

Like trees in the forest our friendship shall endure.

Stitch Count: 25 x 11

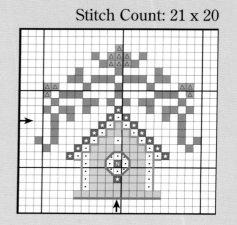

Stitch Count: 48 x 10

Stitch Count: 21 x 20

Stitch Count: 40 x 3

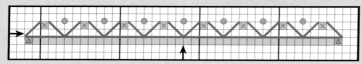

Stitch Count: 38 x 53

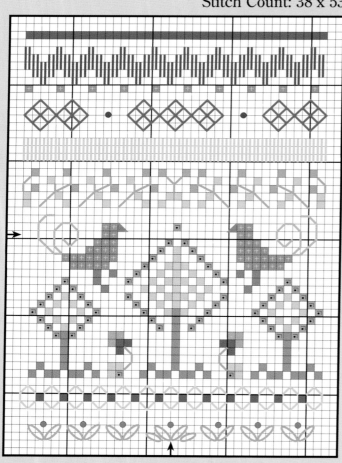

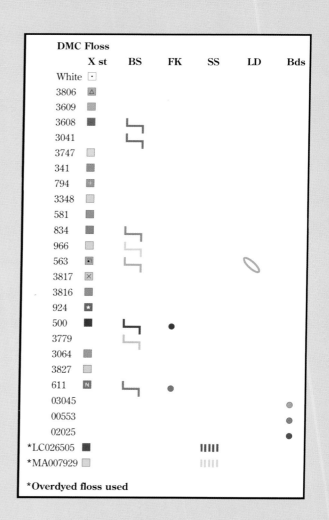

DMC Floss						
	X st	BS	FK	SS	LD	Bds
White	·					
3806	△					
3609						
3608		⌐				
3041		⌐				
3747						
341						
794	+					
3348						
581						
834		⌐				
966		⌐				
563	·	⌐			⬭	
3817	×					
3816						
924	★					
500		⌐	●			
3779		⌐				
3064						
3827						
611	N	⌐	●			
03045						●
00553						●
02025						●
*LC026505				‖‖‖		
*MA007929				‖‖‖		

*Overdyed floss used

Stitch Count: 18 x 19

Stitch Count: 37 x 41

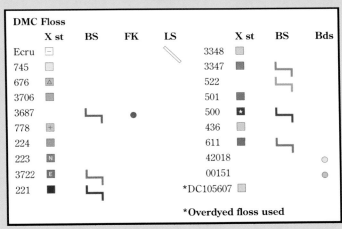

Stitch Count: 38 x 13

Stitch Count: 38 x 53

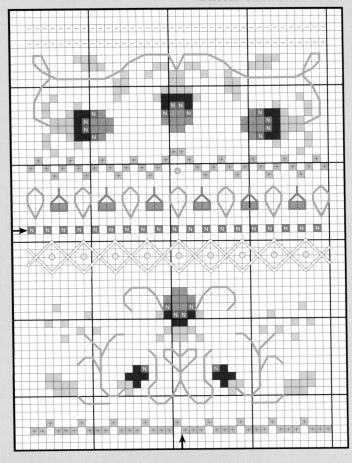

DMC Floss

	X st	BS	FK	LS		X st	BS	Bds
Ecru	⊟				3348			
745					3347		⌐	
676	◬				522		⌐	
3706					501			
3687		⌐	●		500	✶	⌐	
778	+				436			
224					611		⌐	
223	N				42018			○
3722	E	⌐			00151			●
221		⌐			*DC105607			

*Overdyed floss used

Stitch Count: 27 x 27

DMC Floss

	X st	BS	FK		X st	BS	LD
Ecru	–			772			
727				704			
3821	±		●	471	Z		⬭
951				987			
945	◪			3813			
963	◉			563			
760	⊠			964	K		
3706	⠿			959	✳		
894				958			
893	E			3810			
352				502			
351	△		●	501	N		
349			●	3768	✶		
3722				924			
221				739			
327			●	436			
3325				435			
932	⠂			3781			

Stitch Count: 35 x 22

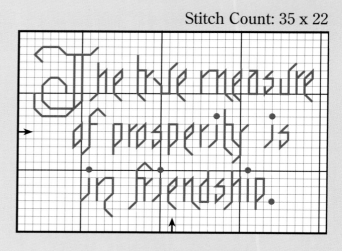

Stitch Count: 26 x 8

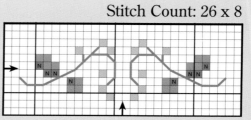

Stitch Count: 7 x 59

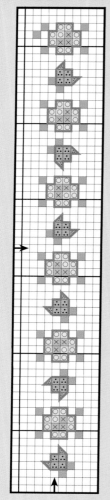

Stitch Count: 58 x 58

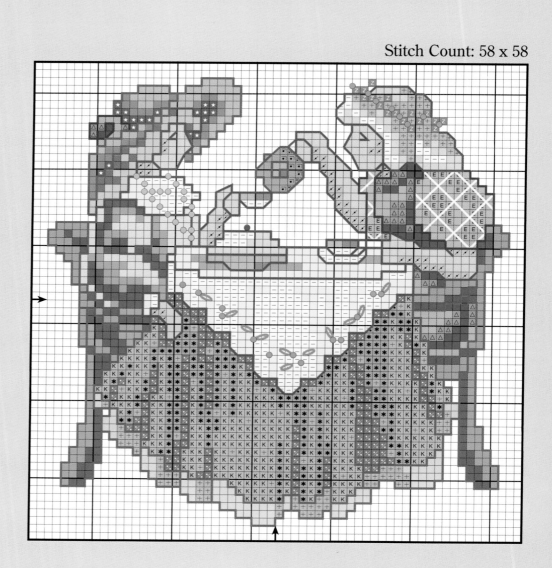

To Have Faith

To every thing
there is a season
and a time
to every purpose
under the heaven.

Eccl. 3:1

DMC Floss

	X st	BS	FK
504	+		
3817			
3816	E		
3815			
500			•

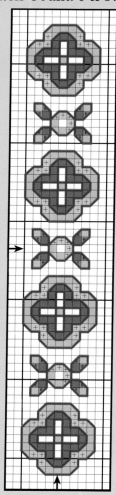

Stitch Count: 66 x 10

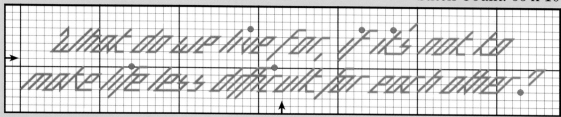

Stitch Count: 40 x 54

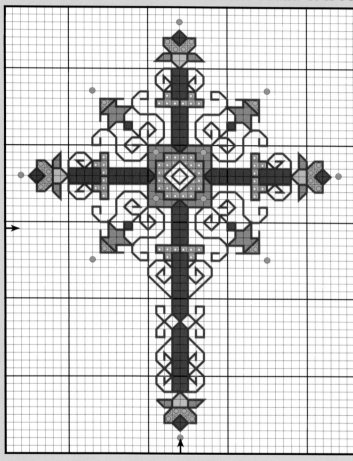

Stitch Count: 22 x 38

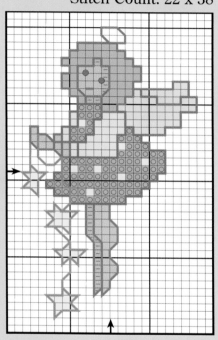

Stitch Count: 34 x 19

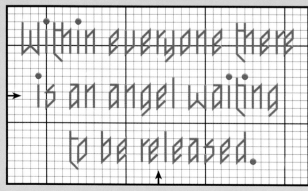

DMC Floss			
	X st	BS	FK
445			
676			
945			
758			
3041			
747			
813			
797			
3807			
336			
772			
993			
3813			
3816			
3815			
3828			
611			

25

MARK 11:9

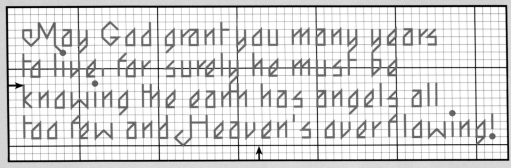

Code for Pages 26-27

DMC Floss

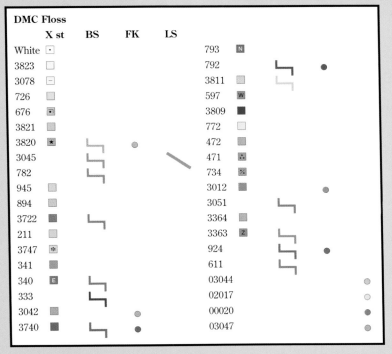

Stitch Count: 19 x 44

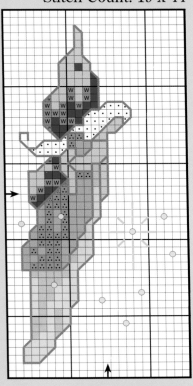

Stitch Count: 22 x 31

Stitch Count: 23 x 25

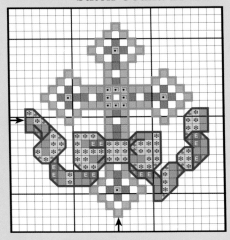

God is my strength and power:
and he maketh my way perfect.
2 SAMUEL 22:33

Stitch Count: 35 x 20

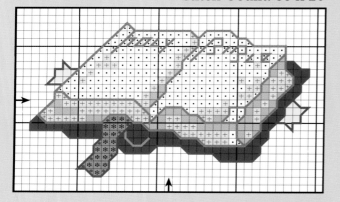

Stitch Count: 17 x 23

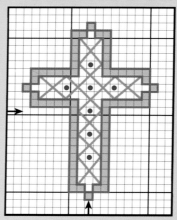

Stitch Count: 13 x 10

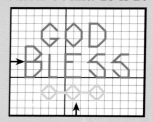

GOD
BLESS

Stitch Count: 33 x 51

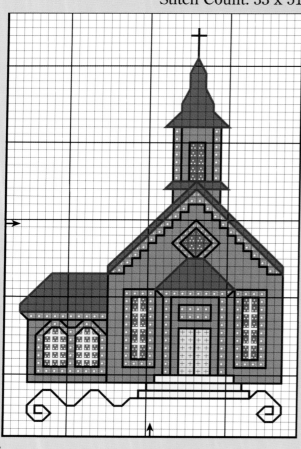

Stitch Count: 34 x 10

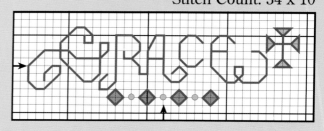

GRACE

DMC Floss

	X st	BS	FK	LS		X st	BS	Bds
White	·				794	※	⌐	
445					3807	■	⌐	
746		⌐			792		⌐	
745	+				930	▦	⌐	
3821					3827		⌐	
3046					834	▦		
3045				/	420		⌐	
3722		⌐			356	■		
221		⌐	●		3787		⌐	
341					03042			●
519			●					

28

Stitch Count: 19 x 28

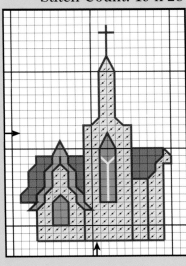

Stitch Count: 24 x 34

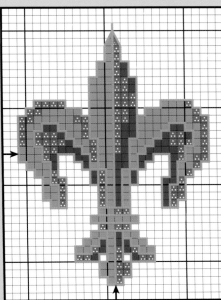

Stitch Count: 18 x 14

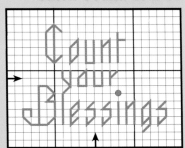

Stitch Count: 24 x 14

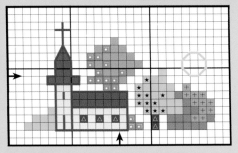

Stitch Count: 28 x 15

Stitch Count: 6 x 30

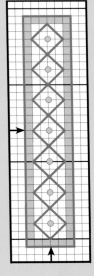

Stitch Count: 22 x 16

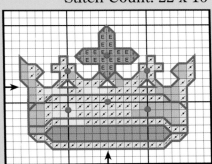

Stitch Count: 25 x 35

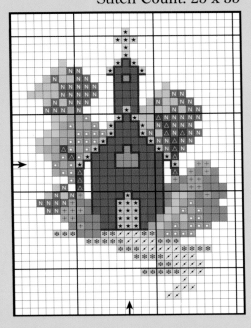

DMC Floss								
	X st	BS	FK		X st	BS	FK	Bds
3823				472				
745				471				
3821				3817			●	
729		⌐		3815	N	⌐		
3727	E			3827	★		⌐	
223		⌐	●	437	✳			
3740		⌐		356				
794				839	△	⌐		
793		⌐		613				
792				611				
3364	+			3021		⌐		
3363				03053				●
3819				02015				●

Stitch Count: 77 x 20

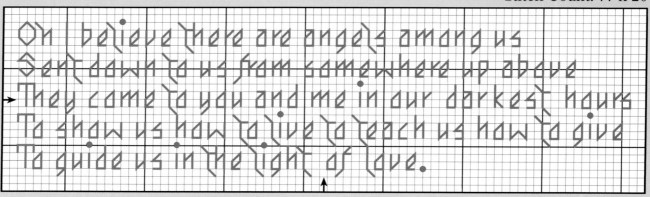

Oh I believe there are angels among us
Sent down to us from somewhere up above
They come to you and me in our darkest hours
To show us how to live to teach us how to give
To guide us in the light of love.

Stitch Count: 38 x 45

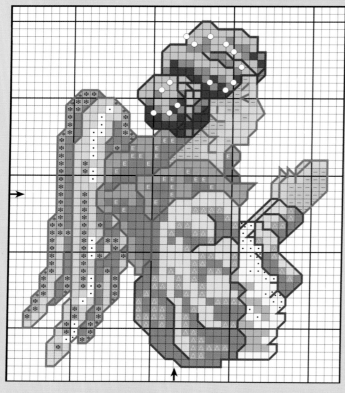

Stitch Count: 26 x 28

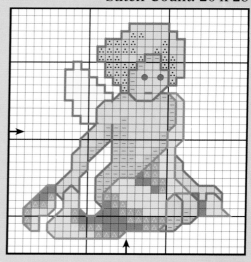

Stitch Count: 12 x 32

Stitch Count: 16 x 27

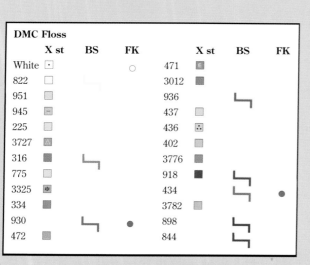

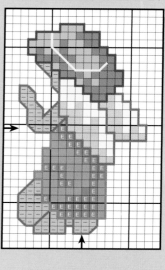

DMC Floss							
	X st	**BS**	**FK**		**X st**	**BS**	**FK**
White	⊡		○	471	E		
822	☐			3012	◪		
951	▦			936		⌐	
945	▬			437	☐		
225	▦			436	⊡		
3727	▲			402	☐		
316	◼	⌐		3776	◪		
775	☐			918	■		
3325	✳			434		⌐	●
334	◼			3782	▦		
930		⌐	●	898		⌐	
472	▦			844		⌐	

Stitch Count: 40 x 40

Stitch Count: 19 x 13

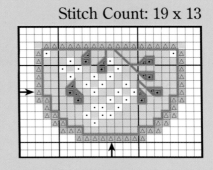

Stitch Count: 24 x 24

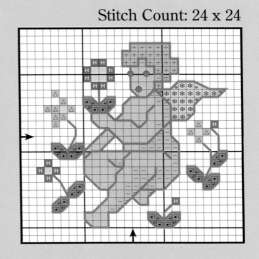

Stitch Count: 22 x 35

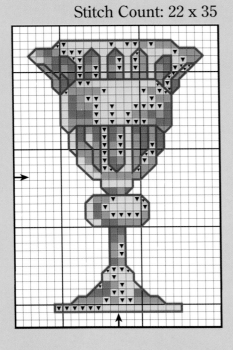

Stitch Count: 40 x 12

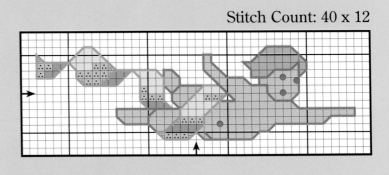

DMC Floss									
	X st	BS		X st	BS		X st	BS	FK
White	·		3803	■		471	·		
727			747	✳		3051		⌐	
725	▼		3761			734	⊞		
676	⊞		813			832	■		
783	■		334	▢		422			
945			793	H		869		⌐	
758	=		336		⌐	3826	■	⌐	
352	△		369			611		⌐	●
963			368	✶		801		⌐	
894	⠿		3363	■					
335		⌐	520	▽					

Stitch Count: 26 x 18

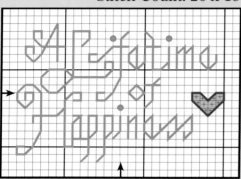

Stitch Count: 18 x 17

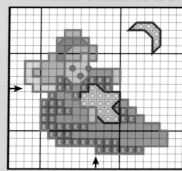

Stitch Count: 18 x 22

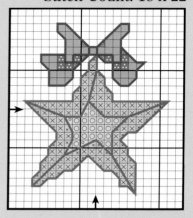

Stitch Count: 16 x 30

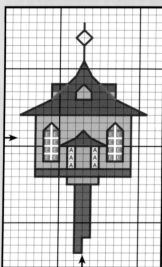

Stitch Count: 55 x 30

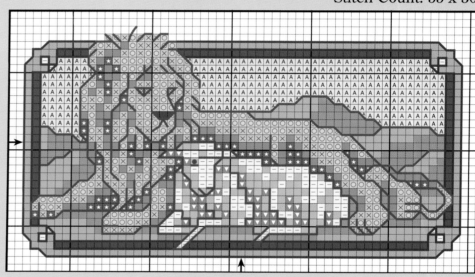

Stitch Count: 25 x 34

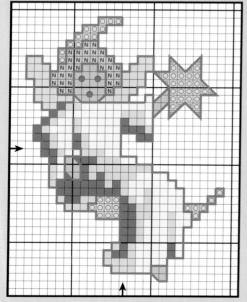

DMC Floss

	X st	BS		X st	BS	FK		X st	BS	FK
Ecru	–		3803	■			3827	N		
3823	A		3608	■			422	■		
676	■		718		⌐		3826	★		
744	○		554	■			434	■	⌐	
725	✕		333	■	⌐		433		⌐	
783	■		775	■			611		⌐	●
945	■		794	■			839	■		●
819	□		793	E			3024	■		
894	+		3363	■		●	3023	▽		
221		⌐	993	■			3021		⌐	
3689	□		943	✸						

Stitch Count: 40 x 23

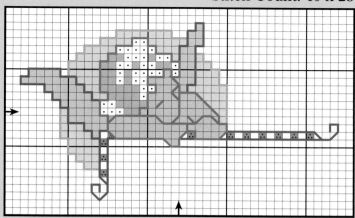

Stitch Count: 22 x 23

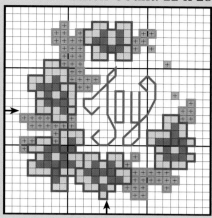

Stitch Count: 54 x 12

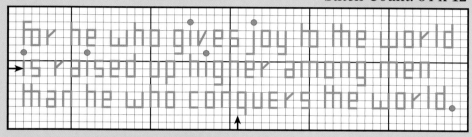

Stitch Count: 13 x 13

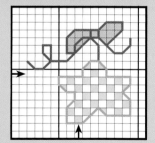

Stitch Count: 41 x 28

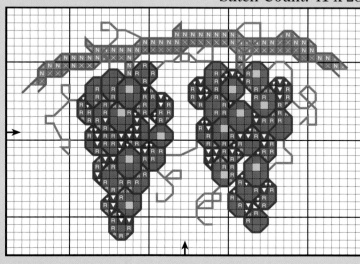

DMC Floss			
	X st	BS	FK
White	⊡		
727	▢		
3820		⌐	
945	▢		
211	▢		
3740		⌐	
3747	▢		
341	▨		
340	◼		
3746	▣		
792	▼		
791		⌐	
470		⌐	
3364	＋		
3363		⌐	
3816		⌐	
3782	▢		
356		⌐	●
3828	N		
420	✕		
869	◼		
611		⌐	

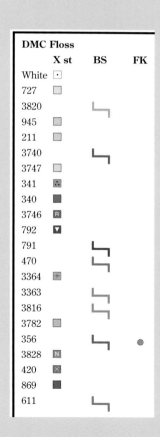

Stitch Count: 31 x 40

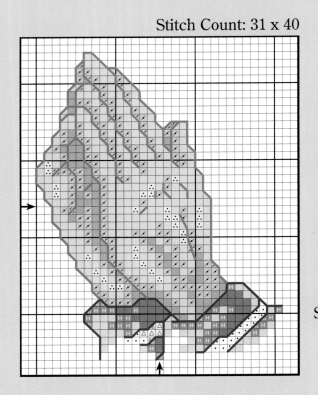

Stitch Count: 20 x 29

Stitch Count: 9 x 55

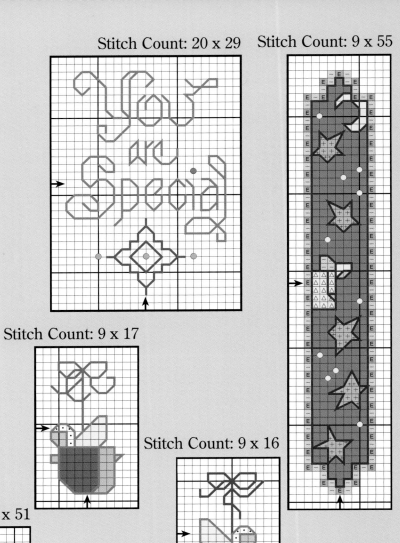

Stitch Count: 9 x 17

Stitch Count: 9 x 16

Stitch Count: 36 x 51

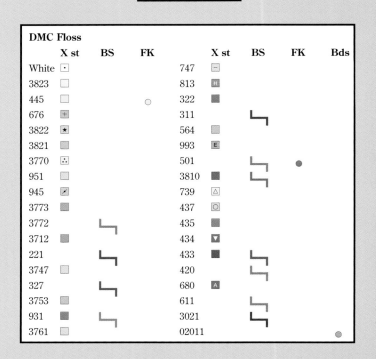

DMC Floss								
	X st	BS	FK		X st	BS	FK	Bds
White	·			747	⊟			
3823				813	H			
445			○	322				
676	+			311		⌐		
3822	★			564				
3821				993	E			
3770				501		⌐	●	
951				3810		⌐		
945	✗			739	△			
3773				437	◎			
3772		⌐		435				
3712				434	▼			
221		⌐		433		⌐		
3747				420		⌐		
327		⌐		680	A			
3753				611		⌐		
931		⌐		3021		⌐		
3761				02011				●

34

To Comfort

Stitch Count: 23 x 28

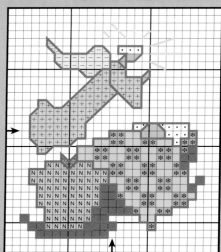

Stitch Count: 24 x 27

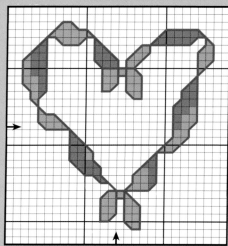

Stitch Count: 54 x 35

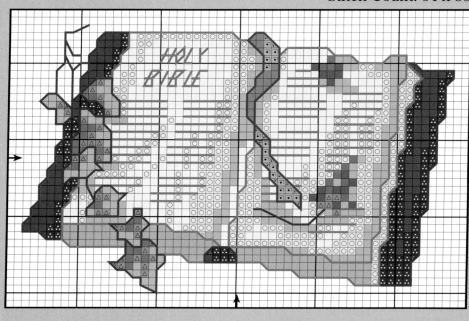

DMC Floss				
	X st	**BS**	**FK**	**LS**
White	·			
746				
3823	−			
727				
677	◯			
676				
945				
352	▨			
3706			●	
3731				
3803		⌐		
209				
3746				
747				
775	+			
519	✳			
598	·			
597				
3807	★			
368	△			
502	△			
501				
500		⌐		
3808		⌐		
3364	E			
422				
420		⌐		
437	N			
435				
356		⌐	●	
611		⌐		
3781				
3031	⊡	⌐		

Stitch Count: 67 x 13

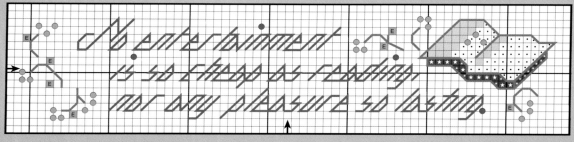

Stitch Count: 28 x 14

Stitch Count: 45 x 8

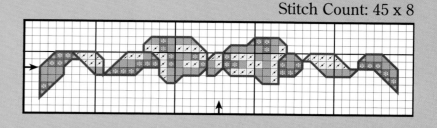

Stitch Count: 13 x 25

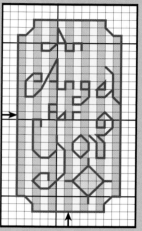

DMC Floss												
	X st	FK	LS		X st	BS	FK		X st	BS	LS
White	⊡		╱	3721		⌐	●	563	⊡		
3078	☐			3727	▪			504	☐		
3047	☐			316	▪			503	⊞		
3045	★			3685		⌐		501		⌐	
951	☐			800	☐			926	▪		
819	✓	○		3755	E			422	Z		
3716	▨			334	▪			420			╱
352	─			3750	▪	⌐		3827	◎		
3712	△			598	N			3830	■		
225	☐			959	▪			842	▪		
223	❋			772	☐			3781	■	⌐	

Stitch Count: 36 x 51

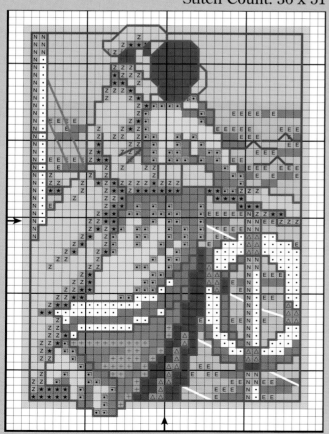

Stitch Count: 39 x 34

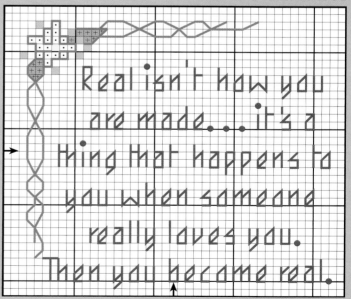

Real isn't how you are made.... it's a thing that happens to you when someone really loves you. Then you become real.

Stitch Count: 72 x 13

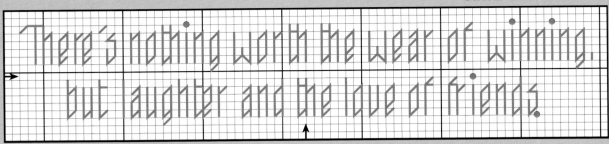

Stitch Count: 34 x 43

Stitch Count: 19 x 19

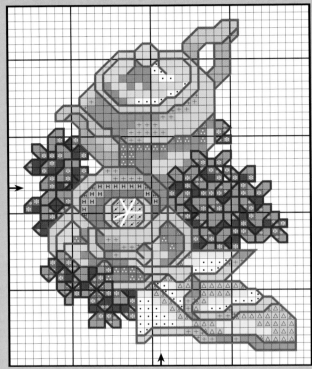

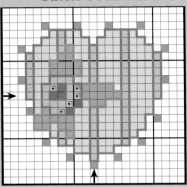

Stitch Count: 13 x 21

Stitch Count: 16 x 15

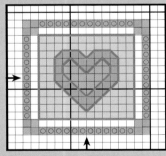

Stitch Count: 24 x 13

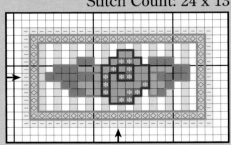

Stitch Count: 16 x 15

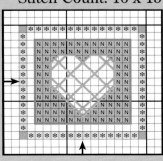

DMC Floss

	X st	BS	FK		X st	BS		X st	BS
White	·			327	■		369		
712	−			550			368	+	
3822				3041			502	■	
3820	■			341	E		739		
307	✻			800	◇		738	△	
727				3761			3827	✎	
3825				3325	N		977	H	
3340				813	■		976	■	
894				322	▦		611		
893	▪			472	■		3781		
3722	■		●	3051	■		3072		
554				3364	◎		648	■	
553	✻			3363			645		

38

Stitch Count: 48 x 7

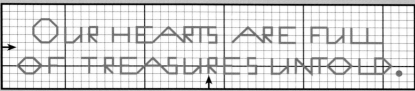

Stitch Count: 17 x 29

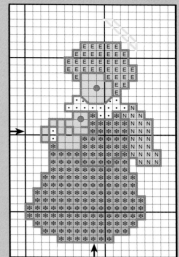

Stitch Count: 10 x 38

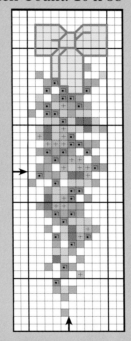

Stitch Count: 28 x 29

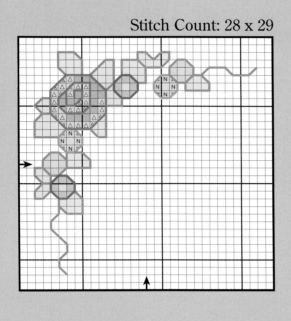

Stitch Count: 18 x 14

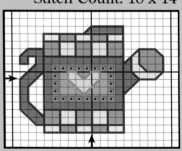

Stitch Count: 42 x 42

DMC Floss						
	X st	BS		X st	BS	FK
White	·		3325	S		
712			799		⌐	
727		⌐	798	✦	⌐	
951			797		⌐	
352	✳		772			
776	△		3363		⌐	
899			472			
309		⌐	471	·|	⌐	
3688			470		⌐	
3803		⌐	937		⌐	
211			3810		⌐	●
210	+		437			
3041		⌐	436	E		
3747	N		611		⌐	●
341		⌐	3021		⌐	
775						

Stitch Count: 66 x 4

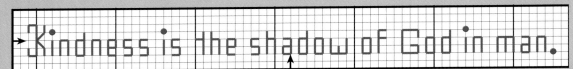

Stitch Count: 41 x 52

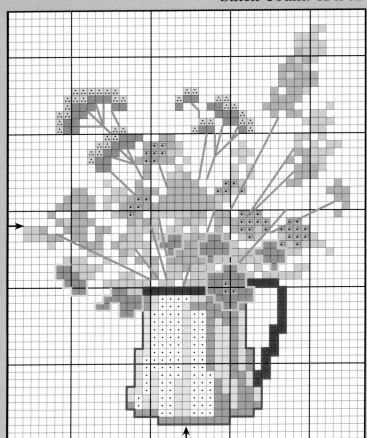

DMC Floss				
	X st	**BS**	**FK**	**Bds**
White	·			
Ecru	–			
445				
775				
3325	+			
3807		⌐	●	
3819				
580		⌐		
504	◎			
3817				
3816	E	⌐		
500		⌐		
436	M			
611		⌐	●	
762				
415				
317				
03055				●
*MA027829	⊡			
*MA036802	⊡			
*MA053901				
*MA0311001				
*LC026505				
*DC105607		⌐		
*MA1211013		⌐		

*Overdyed floss used

Stitch Count: 59 x 4

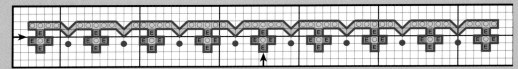

Stitch Count: 63 x 14

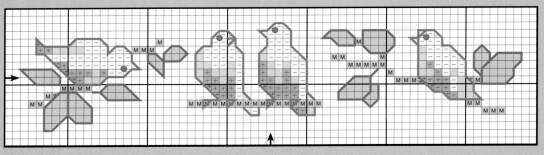

Stitch Count: 21 x 12

Stitch Count: 16 x 29

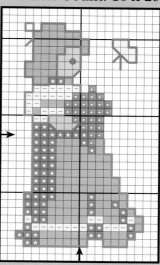

Stitch Count: 49 x 93

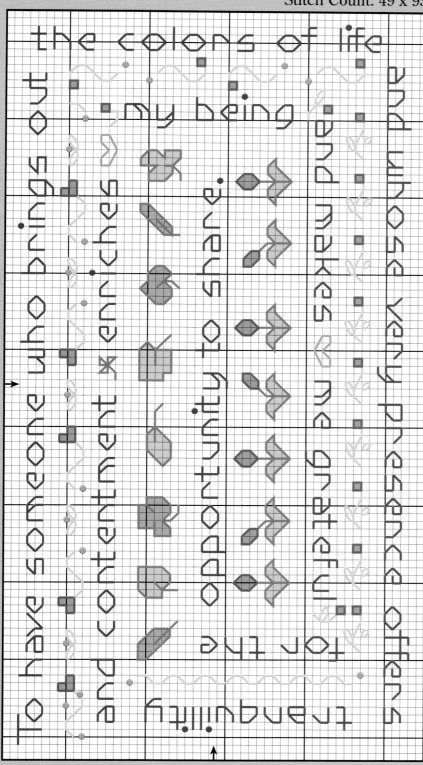

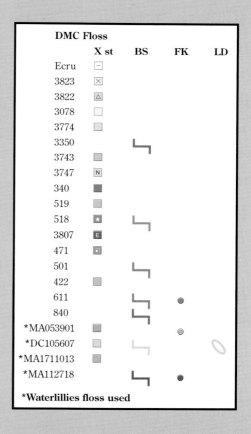

DMC Floss				
	X st	BS	FK	LD
Ecru	–			
3823	⊠			
3822	△			
3078				
3774				
3350		⌐		
3743				
3747	N			
340				
519				
518	★	⌐		
3807	E			
471	⊡			
501		⌐		
422		⌐		
611		⌐⌐	●	
840		⌐⌐	●	
*MA053901			●	
*DC105607		⌐		⬭
*MA1711013				
*MA112718		⌐	●	
Waterlillies floss used				

41

Stitch Count: 58 x 9

Stitch Count: 15 x 27

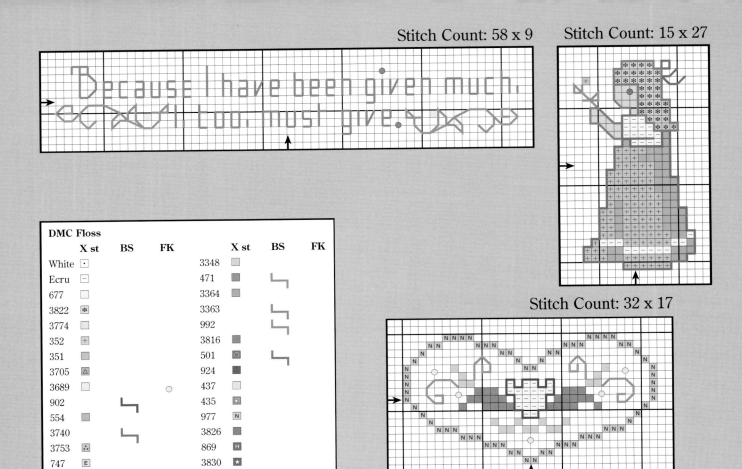

Stitch Count: 32 x 17

DMC Floss

	X st	BS	FK		X st	BS	FK
White	·			3348			
Ecru	−			471		⌐	
677				3364			
3822	✳			3363		⌐	
3774				992		⌐	
352	+			3816			
351				501	◉	⌐	
3705	△			924			
3689			○	437			
902		⌐		435	·		
554		⌐		977	N		
3740		⌐		3826			
3753	⁚			869	H		
747	E			3830	✶		
827				611		⌐	●
518		⌐	●	838	■	⌐	●
312		⌐					

Stitch Count: 55 x 39

Stitch Count: 18 x 40

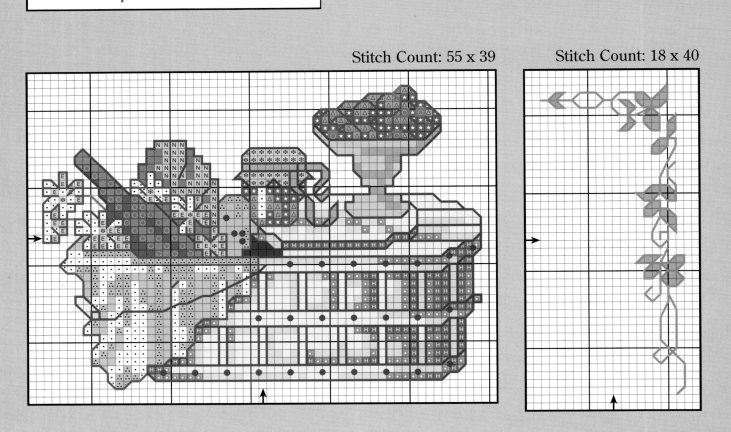

42

Stitch Count: 36 x 21

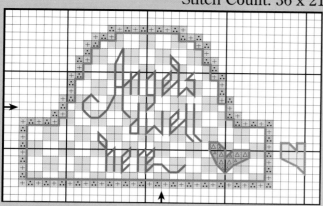

Stitch Count: 23 x 31

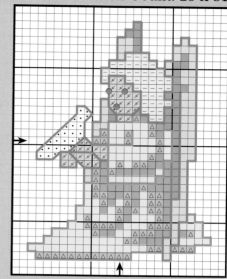

Stitch Count: 19 x 20

Stitch Count: 13 x 18

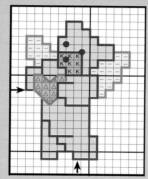

Stitch Count: 26 x 15

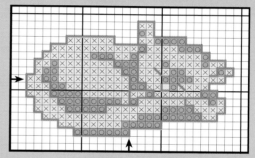

Stitch Count: 34 x 46

DMC Floss					
	X st	BS	X st	BS	FK
White	·		828		
712	×		3811	E	
3823	−		3807		
676			3819		
729			581		
3774			3011		
950			739		
3713			437		
352	△		3827	+	
351			422	K	
350	○		3777		
223			3830		
211			3782		
210	∷		613	◎	
3041			611		●
3609			3021		●
3608			844		
341					

Stitch Count: 35 x 20

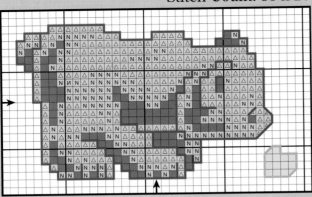

Stitch Count: 38 x 52

Stitch Count: 22 x 28

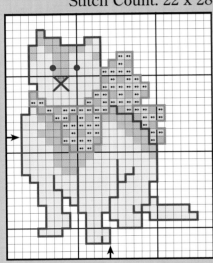

Stitch Count: 27 x 25

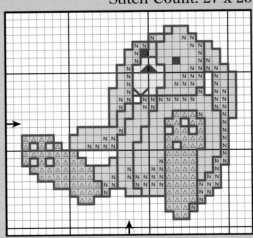

DMC Floss															
	X st	BS		X st	BS		X st	BS	LD		X st	BS	FK
White	·		963			3348				3776			
712			894	+	⌐	989			○	434			
744			3761	••		987	▼	⌐		420			
3820		⌐	519			437				869		⌐	
951			518	★	⌐	436	N			839		⌐	
945	⋇		959	○		3827	△			3024		⌐	
760			992	B		402	E			844		⌐	●
3712	=	⌐	924		⌐								

44

Stitch Count: 33 x 24

In the garden,
after a rainfall
you can faintly, yes,
hear the breaking
of new blooms.

Stitch Count: 28 x 23

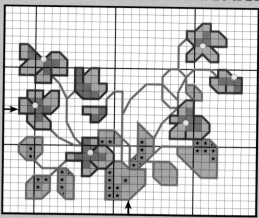

Stitch Count: 19 x 60

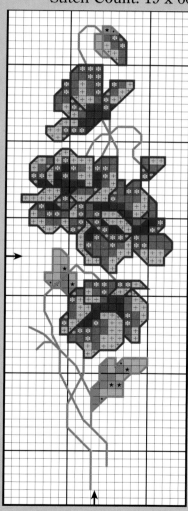

Stitch Count: 29 x 23

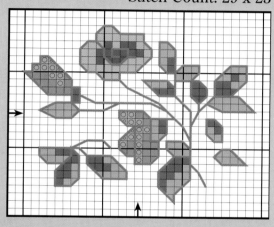

Stitch Count: 10 x 10

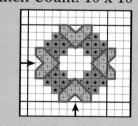

Stitch Count: 13 x 12

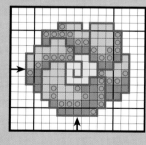

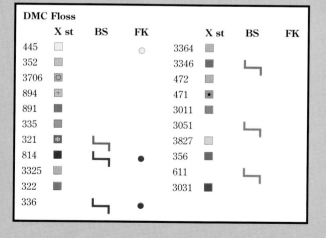

DMC Floss

	X st	BS	FK		X st	BS	FK
445				3364			
352			○	3346		⌐	
3706	◎			472			
894	+			471	★		
891				3011			
335				3051		⌐	
321	✳			3827		⌐	
814		⌐	●	356			
3325				611		⌐	
322				3031			
336		⌐	●				

Stitch Count: 72 x 5

HOLD ON TO YOUR DREAMS FOR EACH
HOLDS ENDLESS POSSIBILITIES.

45

To Be Serene

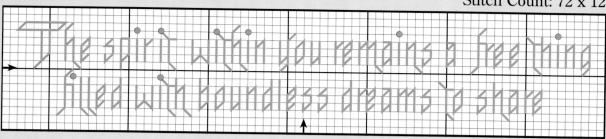

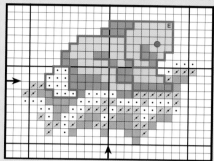

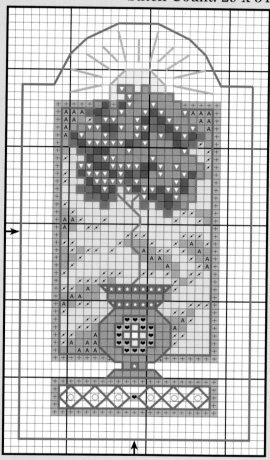

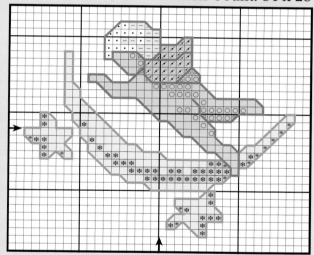

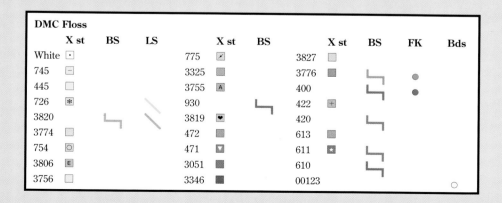

DMC Floss

	X st	BS	LS		X st	BS		X st	BS	FK	Bds
White	·			775	✎		3827				
745	–			3325			3776		⌐	●	
445				3755	A	⌐	400		⌐	●	
726	✳			930		⌐	422	+	⌐		
3820		⌐	/	3819	♥	⌐	420		⌐		
3774				472			613		⌐		
754	◎			471	▼		611	★	⌐		
3806	E			3051			610		⌐		
3756				3346			00123				○

Stitch Count: 44 x 4

Stitch Count: 28 x 30

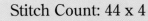

Stitch Count: 39 x 51

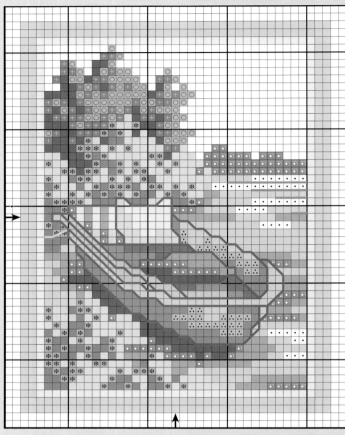

DMC Floss

	X st	BS	FK		X st	BS	FK
White	·			3813	◎		
3823				3816	+	⌐	
744				3815			
352				772			
223	△	⌐	●	368	✳		
3726				320		⌐	
341				472		⌐	
828				3364		⌐	
3325				3363		⌐	
813	◪	⌐		3827		⌐	
930		⌐		437	E	⌐	
3811	◌	⌐		3064			
992		⌐		356		⌐	●

Stitch Count: 76 x 5

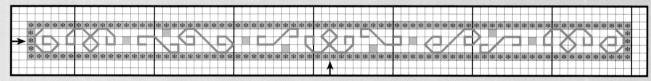

Stitch Count: 23 x 20

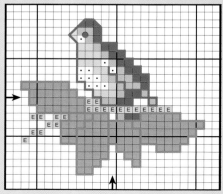

Stitch Count: 40 x 22

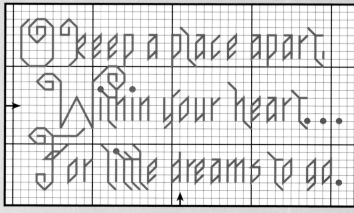

Stitch Count: 56 x 12

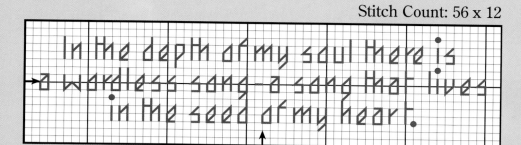

Stitch Count: 17 x 13

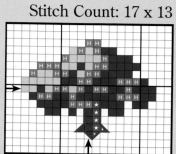

Stitch Count: 68 x 4

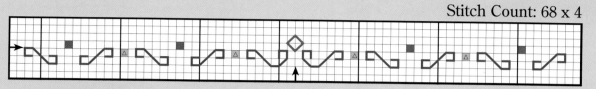

Stitch Count: 78 x 24

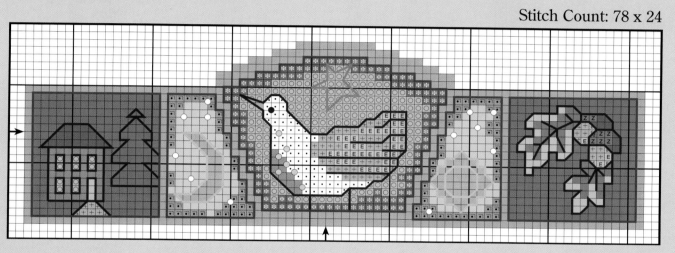

Stitch Count: 35 x 38

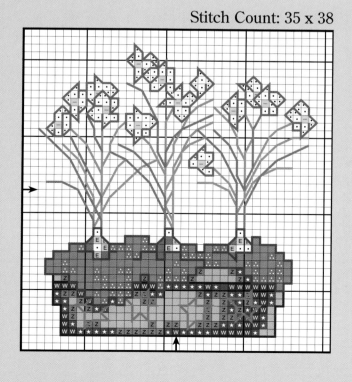

DMC Floss							
	X st	**BS**	**FK**		**X st**	**BS**	**FK**
White	·		○	370			
726	−			581			
676	+			3051		⌐	
3821				504			
352	△			501	H		
351				500			
224				437	E		○
3803		⌐	●	436		⌐	
3746				435			
747				422			
3766				356		⌐	
792		⌐		977		⌐	
931		⌐		976	z	⌐	
3750				975			
3811	○			918	w		
807				301			
562				300		⌐	
3348				839		⌐	
3347				838		⌐	●
372							

Stitch Count: 40 x 53   **Stitch Count: 2 x 44**

Stitch Count: 23 x 36

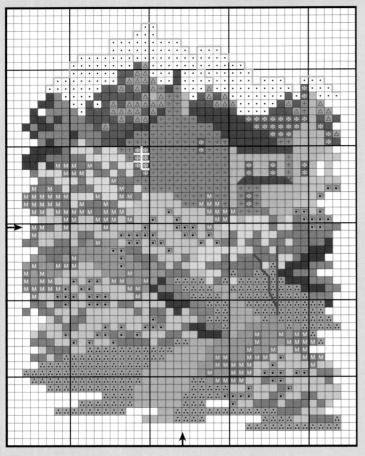

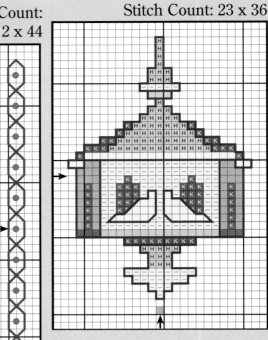

Stitch Count: 20 x 4

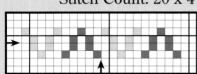

Stitch Count: 18 x 8

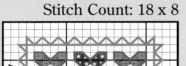

Stitch Count: 47 x 22

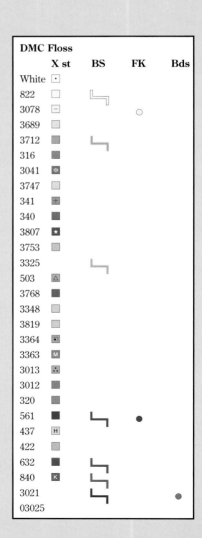

DMC Floss	X st	BS	FK	Bds
White	·			
822		⌐		
3078	−		○	
3689				
3712		⌐		
316				
3041	✳			
3747				
341	+			
340				
3807	✳			
3753		⌐		
3325		⌐		
503	△			
3768				
3348				
3819				
3364	·			
3363	M			
3013	⠇			
3012				
320				
561		⌐	●	
437	H			
422				
632		⌐		
840	K	⌐		
3021		⌐		●
03025				

50

Stitch Count: 40 x 54

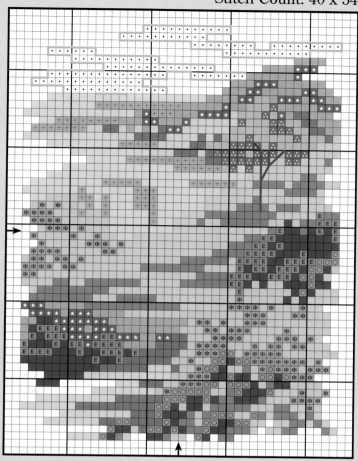

DMC Floss

	X st	BS	FK
White	·		
3824			
352	△		●
3712	◎		
3326			
3722			
3830			
747			
3325	+	⌐	
3807		⌐	●
3819			
3348			
472			
471	N		
3012			
3364	✳		
3363			
3346		⌐	
503			
3768	★		
320	E		
561			
437			
435			
422			
356	·	⌐	
611		⌐	
839		⌐	

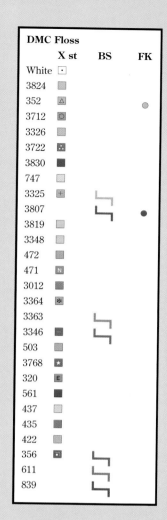

Stitch Count: 29 x 16

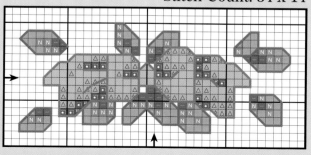

We take for granted
the very things
that most deserve
our gratitude.

Stitch Count: 38 x 34

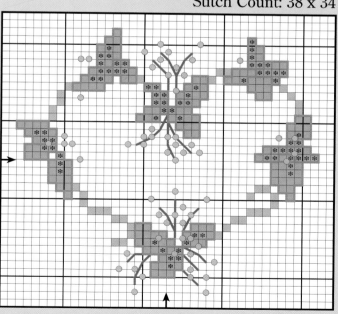

Stitch Count: 34 x 14

Stitch Count: 38 x 54

Stitch Count: 14 x 38

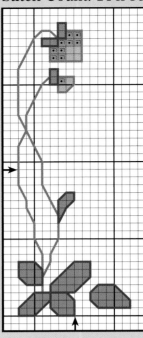

Stitch Count: 12 x 36

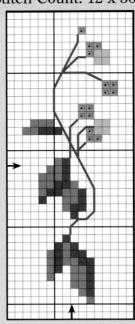

Stitch Count: 12 x 41

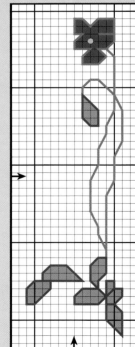

Stitch Count: 47 x 8

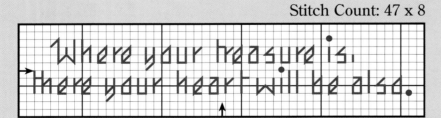

Where your treasure is,
there your heart will be also.

Stitch Count: 19 x 18

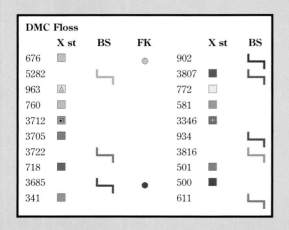

DMC Floss						
	X st	**BS**	**FK**		**X st**	**BS**
676	▦		●	902		
5282		⌐		3807	■	⌐
963	△			772	▫	
760	▦			581	▦	
3712	▪			3346	▦	
3705	▦			934		⌐
3722	▦	⌐		3816	▦	⌐
718	▦			501	▦	
3685	▦	⌐	●	500	■	⌐
341	▦			611		⌐

Stitch Count: 38 x 48

Stitch Count: 25 x 47

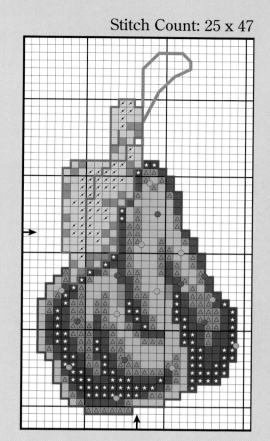

Stitch Count: 43 x 16

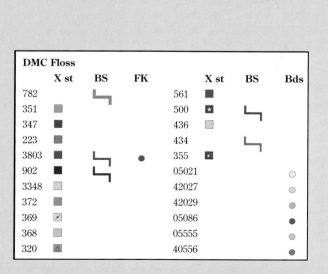

Stitch Count: 22 x 45

DMC Floss

	X st	BS	FK		X st	BS	Bds
782				561			
351				500			
347				436			
223				434			
3803			●	355			
902				05021			
3348				42027			○
372				42029			○
369				05086			●
368				05555			○
320				40556			●

Stitch Count: 32 x 24

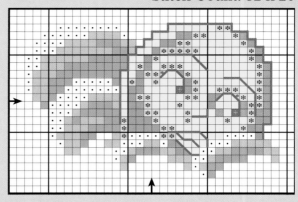

Stitch Count: 32 x 20

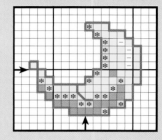

Stitch Count: 57 x 32

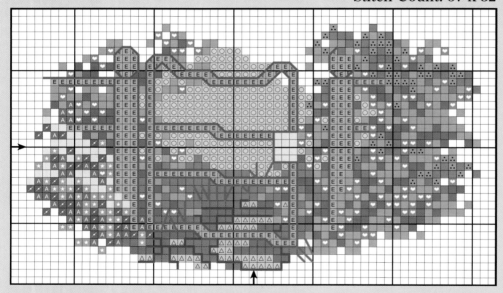

Stitch Count: 14 x 12

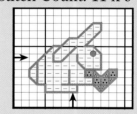

Stitch Count: 11 x 9

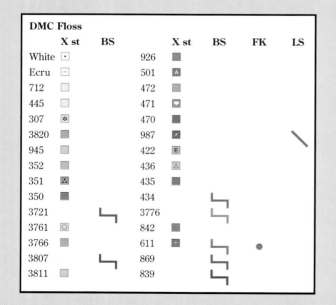

Stitch Count: 21 x 31

DMC Floss						
	X st	BS		X st	BS	FK	LS
White	·		926			
Ecru	–		501	A		
712			472			
445			471	♥		
307	✳		470			
3820			987	✒		
945			422	E		
352			436	△		
351	∴		435			
350			434			
3721		⌐	3776		⌐	
3761	○		842			
3766			611	✛	⌐	●
3807		⌐	869		⌐	
3811			839		⌐	

Stitch Count: 40 x 19

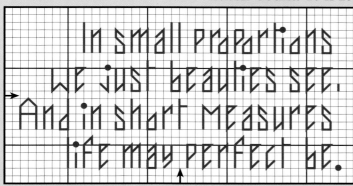

Stitch Count: 19 x 30

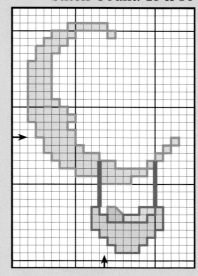

Stitch Count: 25 x 17

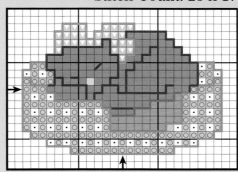

DMC Floss							
	X st	BS	FK		X st	BS	LS	Bds
White	·			471	A		
745	+			470			
727				3011			
725				924			
783				3827	◎		
781				3776	✳		
3045				611	❋		
945				3072			
963				648	✦		
747				646			
336		●		844			
472				02003			○

Stitch Count: 33 x 40

Stitch Count: 23 x 36

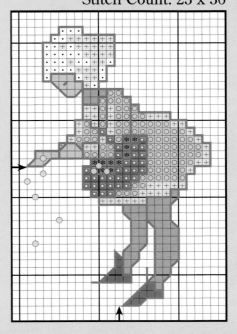

Stitch Count: 47 x 26

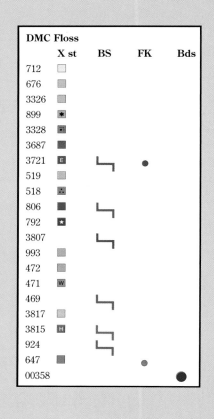

Kind words produce their own image on mens souls, and a beautiful image it is. They sooth, and quiet, and comfort the listener.

Stitch Count: 13 x 13

Stitch Count: 15 x 15

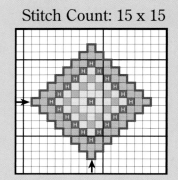

Stitch Count: 15 x 15

DMC Floss

	X st	BS	FK	Bds
712				
676				
3326				
899				
3328				
3687				
3721	E	⌐	●	
519				
518				
806		⌐		
792				
3807		⌐		
993				
472				
471	W			
469		⌐		
3817				
3815	H	⌐		
924		⌐		
647			●	
00358				●

Stitch Count: 44 x 44

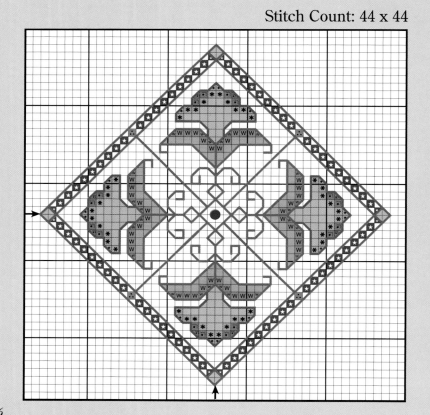

Stitch Count: 18 x 21

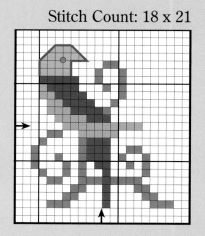

To Have Joy

Stitch Count: 26 x 31

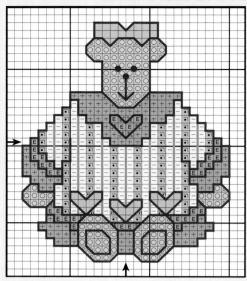

Stitch Count: 32 x 28

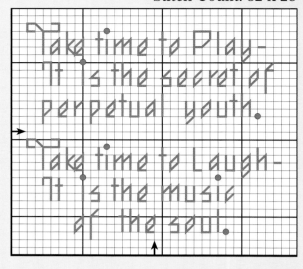

Stitch Count: 20 x 21

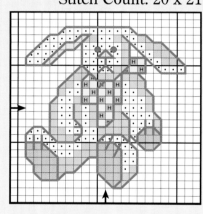

Stitch Count: 16 x 3

DMC Floss							
	X st	BS	FK		X st	BS	FK
White	·			341	△		
Ecru	—			799		⌐	
445				793	■		
729		⌐		772			
945				472			
3824	·			3364	··		
3713				993	N		
894				959	E		
893	H			3815		⌐	
352				3827	○		
351				436	✕		
3722		⌐	●	422			
3041		⌐		839		⌐	●
828				611		⌐	●
3325	+			3021		⌐	●

Stitch Count: 21 x 35

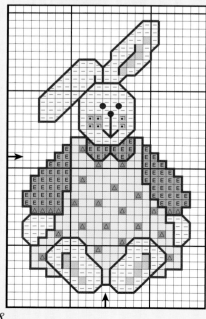

Stitch Count: 21 x 26

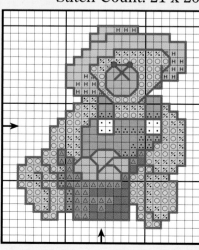

Stitch Count: 23 x 29

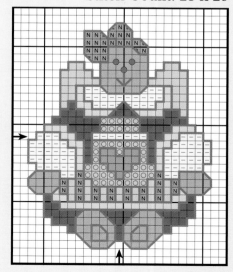

Stitch Count: 76 x 11

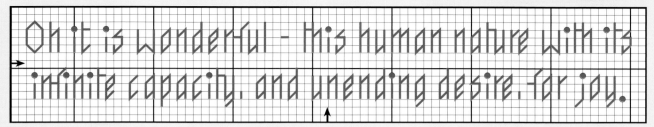

Stitch Count: 47 x 24

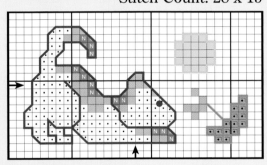

Stitch Count: 20 x 27

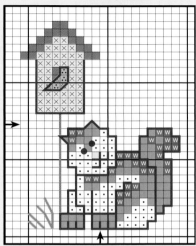

Stitch Count: 28 x 15

Stitch Count: 19 x 10

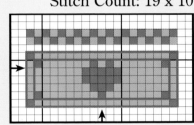

Stitch Count: 16 x 16

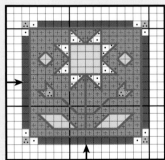

Stitch Count: 16 x 15

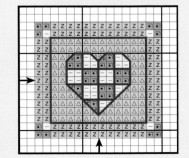

DMC Floss								
	X st	BS		X st	BS	FK	X st	BS	FK
White	·		553				3364	·	
Ecru	–		3608				3363		
3823	⊠		3740				924		
744			341	+			3827	z	
743	◉		775	△			435		
742			519				415		
976			3807				318	w	
3713			3811				844		●
760	⊡		807				3024		
352			806	✳		●	647	N	
210			772				3021		●

59

Stitch Count: 24 x 55

Stitch Count: 46 x 40

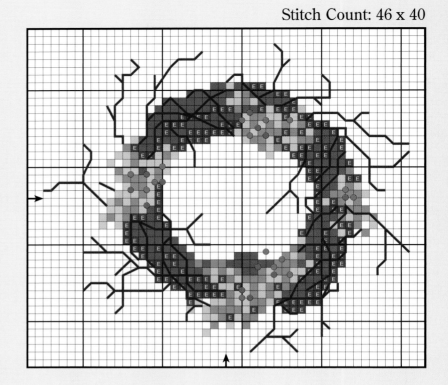

Stitch Count: 23 x 57

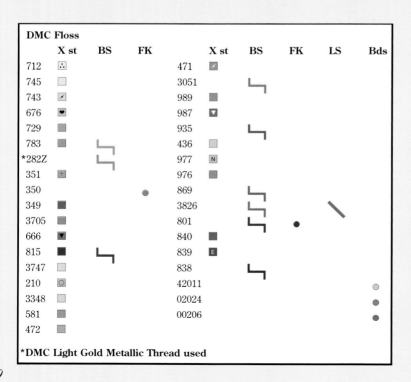

DMC Floss								
	X st	BS	FK	X st	BS	FK	LS	Bds
712	⠢			471				
745				3051		⌐		
743				989				
676	♥			987	▼			
729				935		⌐		
783		⌐		436				
*282Z		⌐		977	N			
351	+			976				
350			●	869		⌐		
349				3826		⌐		
3705				801		⌐	●	
666	▼			840				/
815		⌐		839	E			
3747				838		⌐		
210	◎			42011				○
3348				02024				●
581				00206				●
472								

*DMC Light Gold Metallic Thread used

60

Stitch Count: 19 x 31

Stitch Count: 14 x 35

Stitch Count: 28 x 36

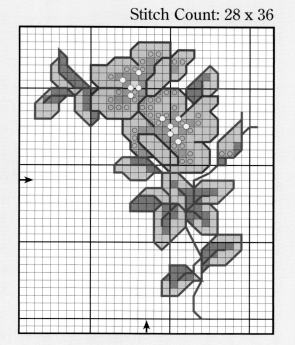

Stitch Count: 35 x 5

Stitch Count: 20 x 19

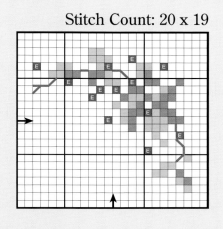

Stitch Count: 40 x 51

Earth laughs in flowers.

DMC Floss							
	X st	BS	FK		X st	BS	FK
Ecru	☐	\	○	3807		⌐	●
744	☐			791		⌐	●
945	☐			3819	☐		
353	☐			3348	☐		
352	◎			3347	☐		
351	☐			3346		⌐	
3712	+			3345		⌐	
815		⌐		472	△		
3687	E			3051		⌐	
3608	☐			581	☐		
3803		⌐		436	N		
340	▣			3782	☐		
809	⣿			611	☐		●
794	☐			3021		⌐	

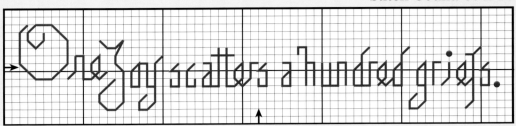

Stitch Count: 60 x 11

Stitch Count: 34 x 47

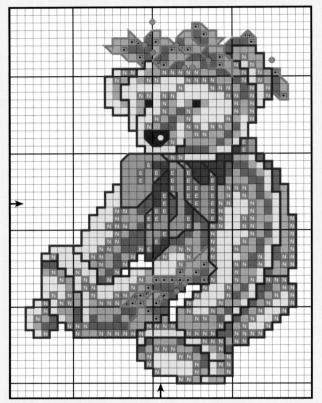

Stitch Count: 34 x 21

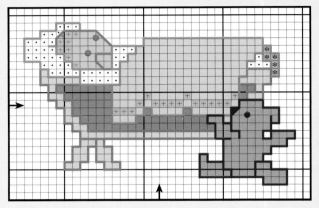

Stitch Count: 22 x 21

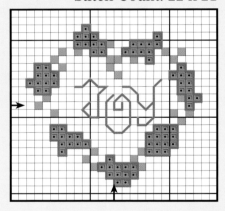

Stitch Count: 24 x 31

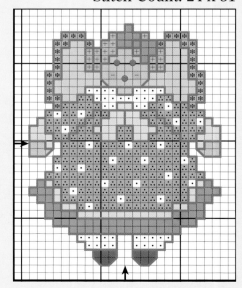

DMC Floss								
	X st	BS	FK		X st	BS	FK	Bds
White	·			518		⌐		
676	+			793				
3045		⌐		472				
945				471	·			
758	−			3051		⌐		
963				3346				
351				543			○	
210	∴			437				
554				611		⌐	●	
553	E			842	N			
327				841				
550		⌐	●	840				
747				838		⌐	●	
519	✳			00553				●

Stitch Count: 19 x 16

Stitch Count: 13 x 18

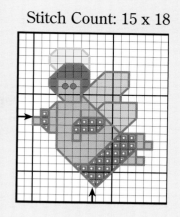

Stitch Count: 15 x 18

Stitch Count: 32 x 10

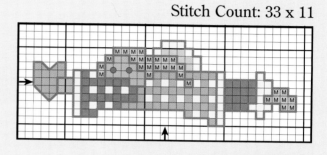

Stitch Count: 33 x 11

Stitch Count: 34 x 60

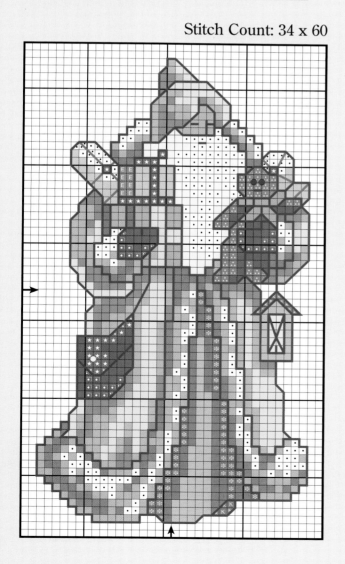

Stitch Count: 28 x 24

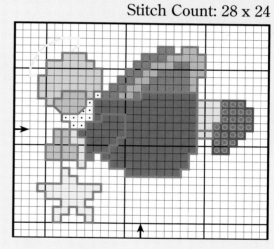

DMC Floss						
	X st	**BS**		**X st**	**BS**	**FK**
White	·		368			
745			3816			
445		⌐	3348			
3822	+		471			
3821			3012	※		
783			822			○
950			436	M		
3706			976	※		
3607			3826		⌐	
718	✶	⌐	611	G	⌐	●
341	E		3024			
340			3023			
3746	·		3790	K		
775			3031		⌐	●

Stitch Count: 42 x 37

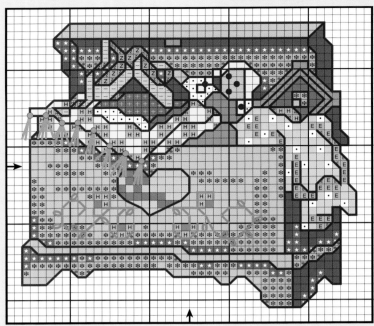

Stitch Count: 20 x 22

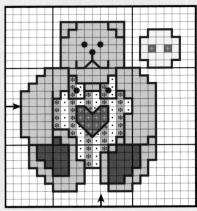

Stitch Count: 23 x 22

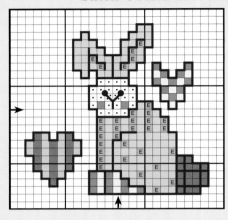

Stitch Count: 26 x 4

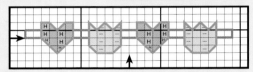

Stitch Count: 50 x 45

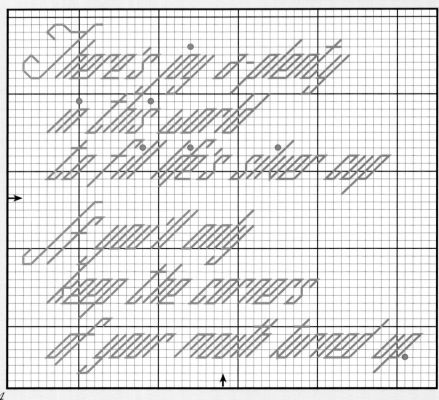

DMC Floss					
	X st	BS	FK	LS	LD
White	·				
3078					
3820			●	/	
951					
3825	H				
225	−				
3326	Z				
892					
3689					
316		⌐	●		
747					
519	E				
794					
340	+				
471		⌐			0
3053					
437					
436	✳				
435	★				
869					
842					
838		⌐	●		

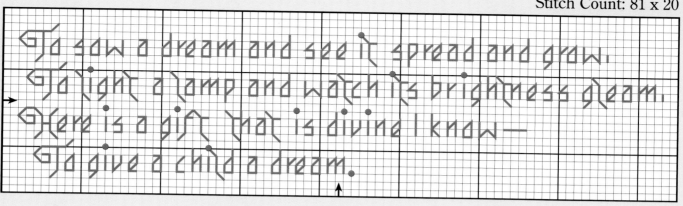

To sow a dream and see it spread and grow,
To light a lamp and watch its brightness gleam,
Here is a gift that is divine I know—
To give a child a dream.

Stitch Count: 62 x 45

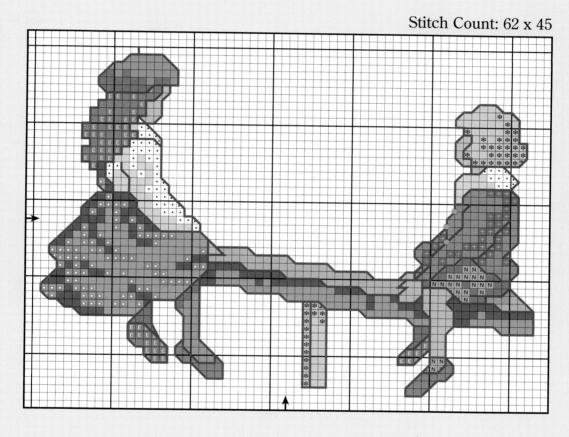

DMC Floss					
	X st	FK	X st	BS	FK
White	·		471		
727	◎		503		
676			502	✳	
3820		●	3815	⌐	●
945			3768		
3733			437		
223	✛		436	✳	
3727			356		
316			680		
3761			612		
3755	N		3790	E	
334			3781		⌐

Stitch Count: 21 x 18

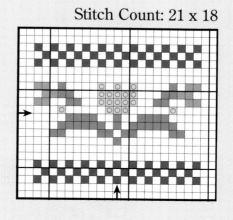

Stitch Count: 33 x 42

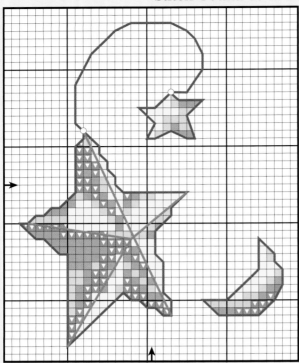

DMC Floss

	X st	BS	FK	LS	LD	Bds
White	·					
712						
3078						
745	−					
445	◎					
726						
3820		⌐				
783	▽					
781						
945				/		
3716						
350						
3721		⌐⌐			◌	
327	■	⌐⌐	•			
747						
340						
472						
471	⟋					
3051		⌐				
3346	■					
3816						
924	E	⌐⌐				
433		⌐⌐				
3371		⌐⌐				
3021		⌐⌐				
00123						○

Stitch Count: 9 x 55

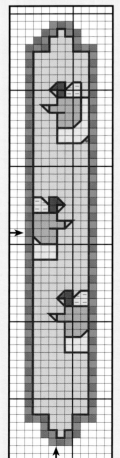

Stitch Count: 24 x 46

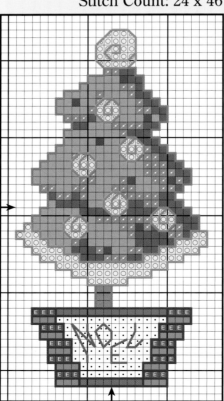

Stitch Count: 25 x 38

Stitch Count: 40 x 26

Stitch Count: 27 x 31

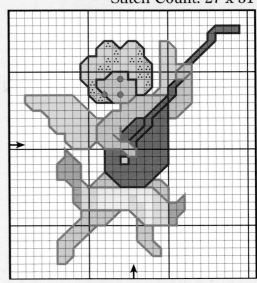

Stitch Count: 37 x 39

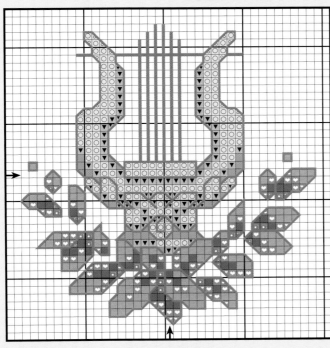

DMC Floss

	X st	BS	LS		X st	BS	FK
Ecru	–			3760		⌐	
3823	☐			793	■		
745	◎	·		3807		⌐	●
727	☐			3750		⌐	●
725	✱			472	■		
3820	■			471	♥		
676	▼		╱	3051		⌐	
729	■			3346	■		
783	■			437	☐		
3829	■	⌐	╱	436	∴		
945	☐			3827	+		
3608	■			3776	E		
3803	■	⌐		611	■	⌐	●
747	☐			801	■	⌐	
519	✱			3021	■	⌐	

Stitch Count: 16 x 29

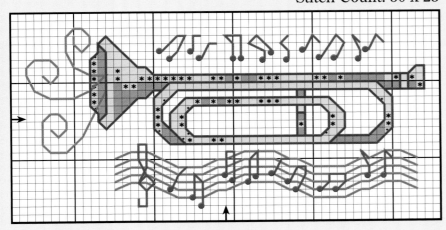

Stitch Count: 50 x 23

Stitch Count: 27 x 27

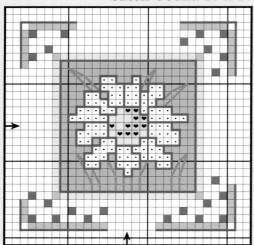

Stitch Count: 23 x 56

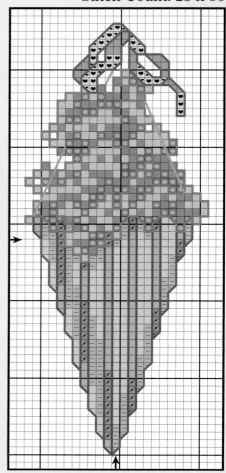

Stitch Count: 34 x 54

Stitch Count: 36 x 9

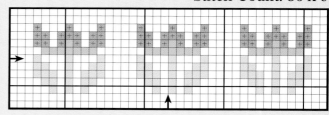

DMC Floss													
	X st	LS	X st	BS	X st	BS	X st	BS	X st	BS	X st	BS
White	·		776		3803		772		3011			
445			760	+	902		3348	○	520			
307	♥		352		3740		472		989	★		
3822			351		519		471	▼	987			
3821	−		349		340		3819		869			
3820			3687		3746	A	581					

How do you say 'Thank You'
to the angels above
Who've blessed your life
with their magical love?

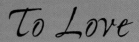

LOVE BEGAN IN A GARDEN

Stitch Count: 40 x 41

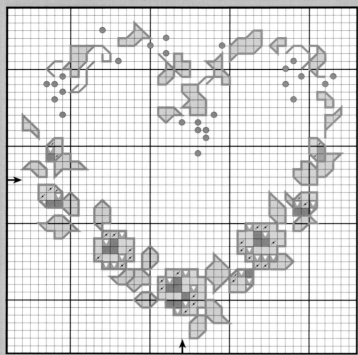

Stitch Count: 15 x 19

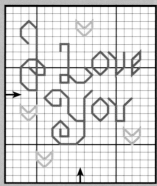

Stitch Count: 30 x 27

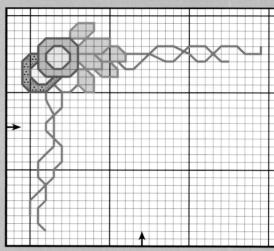

Stitch Count: 29 x 25

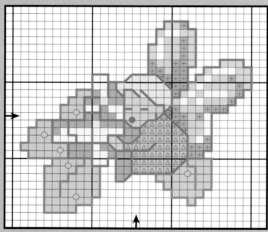

Stitch Count: 23 x 32

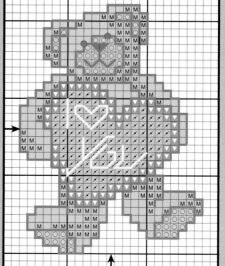

DMC Floss						
	X st	BS		X st	BS	FK
Ecru			3803			
745			3041			
3822			775			
676			3325			
3774			3811			
353			959			
3712			3348			
3328			3347			
819			3827			
3716			436			
3806			611			

Stitch Count: 66 x 12

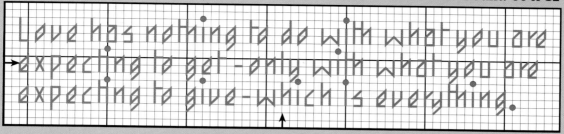

Stitch Count: 36 x 26

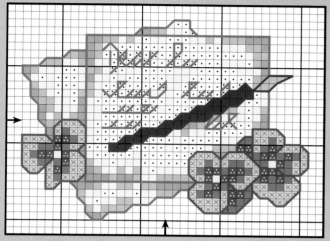

Stitch Count: 34 x 32

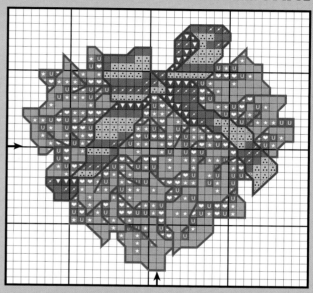

Stitch Count: 24 x 17

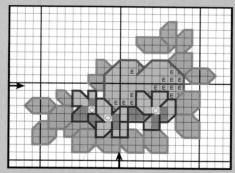

Stitch Count: 26 x 26

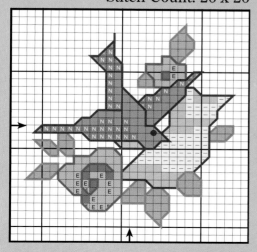

DMC Floss

	X st	BS		X st	BS	FK
White	·		340	■		
3823	–		813	■		
3078	□		322	N		
445	⊙		792	▦		
676	■		791		⌐	
729	■		3364	■		
3716	■		3346	U		
3806	E		472	■		
3688	⠢		471	★		
3687	■		3051	▽		
3803	◪		935		⌐	
3685	▼	⌐	356		⌐	●
902		⌐	610		⌐	
210	■		3024	■		
553	■		844	■	⌐	
3747	⊠		3021		⌐	●

71

Stitch Count: 15 x 13

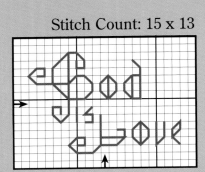

Stitch Count: 17 x 7

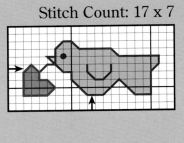

Stitch Count: 13 x 11

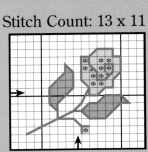

Stitch Count: 9 x 10

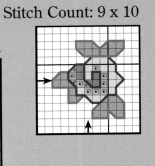

Stitch Count: 19 x 19

Stitch Count: 42 x 47

Stitch Count: 12 x 17

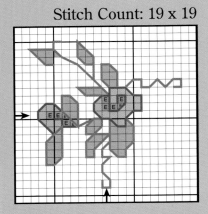

Stitch Count: 32 x 25

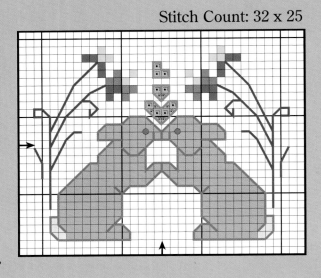

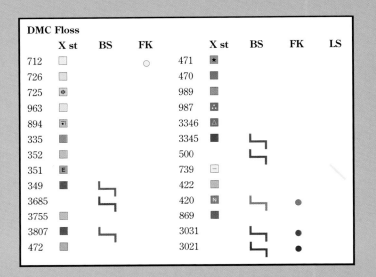

DMC Floss								
	X st	BS	FK		X st	BS	FK	LS
712			○	471	★			
726				470				
725	✳			989				
963				987	▨			
894	▪			3346	△			
335				3345				
352				500		⌐		
351	E			739	⊟			
349		⌐		422				
3685		⌐		420	N	⌐	●	
3755				869				
3807		⌐		3031		⌐	●	
472		⌐		3021			●	

Stitch Count: 44 x 26

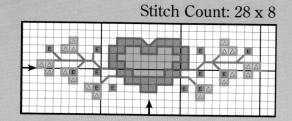

Stitch Count: 27 x 25

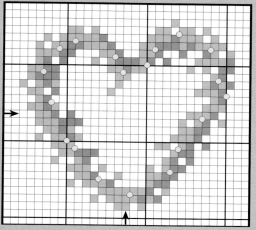

Stitch Count: 21 x 21

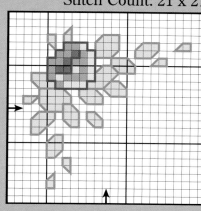

Stitch Count: 44 x 56

DMC Floss					
	X st	BS	FK	LS	Bds
818					
3354					
3731					
3803					
3726			●		
3811	△				
813					
772					
368					
320					
3813					
3816	E				
3815					
739					
437	+				
435					
3827					
3064					
3781					
02018					○

Stitch Count: 19 x 17

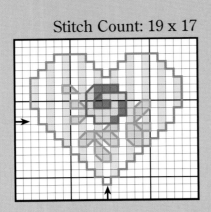

Stitch Count: 19 x 17

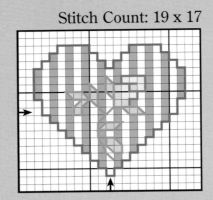

Stitch Count: 19 x 17

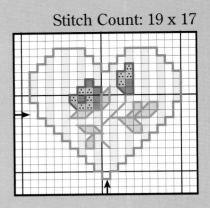

Stitch Count: 58 x 10

DMC Floss									
	X st	BS		X st	BS	FK	X st	BS	Bds
White	·		3722	◪			3807		
445			221		⌐		3348		
948			333		⌐		581		
3778	▨		341	▨	⌐		368		
3689	+		3041				3827		
3688			3761				356		
894		⌐	828	△			02019		○
3806	⊡		799		⌐	●	00431		●

Stitch Count: 36 x 36

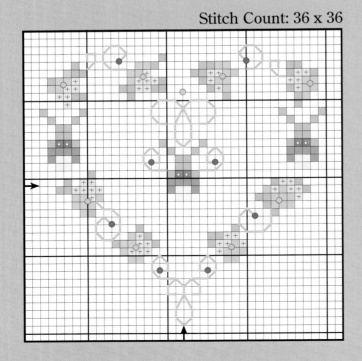

Stitch Count: 30 x 32

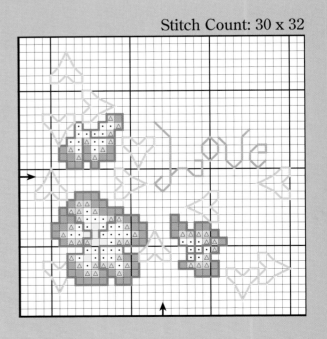

Stitch Count: 28 x 16

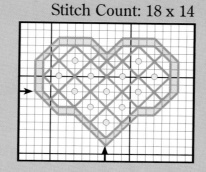

Stitch Count: 18 x 14

Stitch Count: 19 x 25

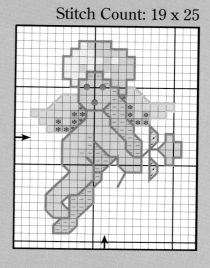

Stitch Count: 46 x 43

Stitch Count: 24 x 26

Stitch Count: 20 x 27

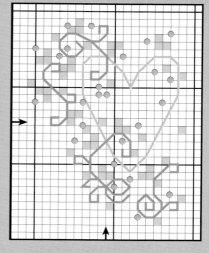

DMC Floss							
	X st	BS	FK	X st	BS	FK	Bds
712	◎			519	✳		
3823				793			
727				772	✎		
725	+			966			
676	⁙			3816			
3045		⌐		3815			
3774				3827			
754	−			3776	■		
760				356		⌐	
3712		⌐		611		⌐	●
3706	△			839		⌐	●
221		⌐	●	02002			○
3747				00275			●
747							

Stitch Count: 37 x 12

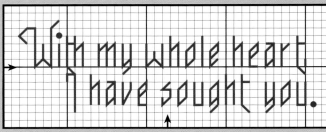

Stitch Count: 18 x 36

Stitch Count: 13 x 28

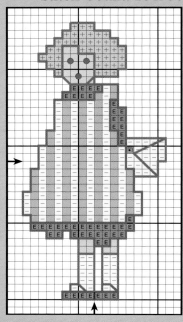

Stitch Count: 43 x 38

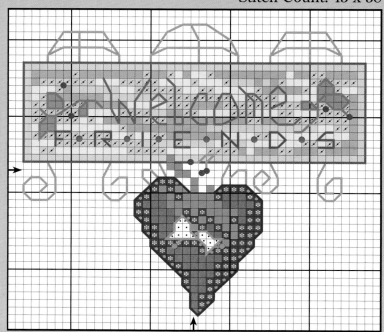

Stitch Count: 23 x 26

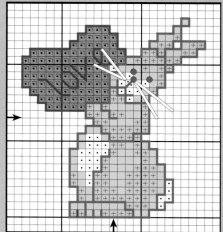

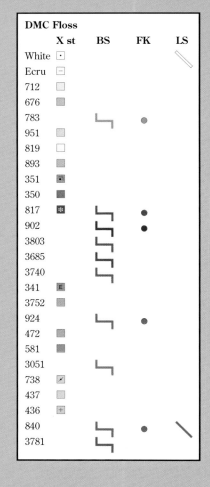

Stitch Count: 16 x 35

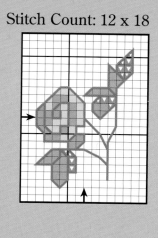

Stitch Count: 12 x 18

Stitch Count: 29 x 27

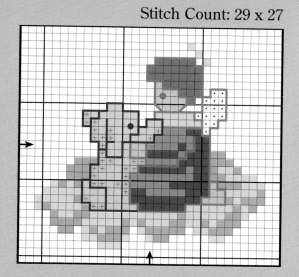

Stitch Count: 37 x 23

There is a silence born of love, which expresses everything.

Stitch Count: 37 x 53

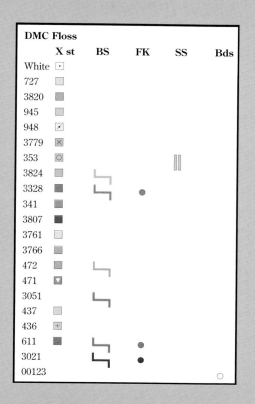

DMC Floss	X st	BS	FK	SS	Bds
White	·				
727					
3820					
945					
948	✎				
3779	✕				
353	◎			‖	
3824		⌐			
3328		⌐	●		
341					
3807					
3761					
3766					
472		⌐			
471	▼				
3051		⌐			
437					
436	+				
611		⌐	●		
3021		⌐	●		
00123					○

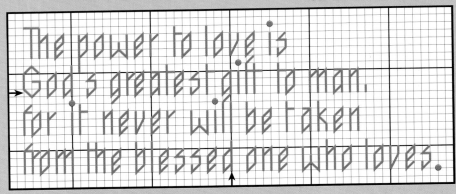

The power to love is God's greatest gift to man, for it never will be taken from the blessed one who loves.

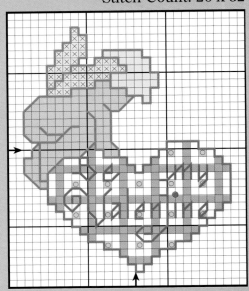

DMC Floss

	X st	BS		X st	BS	FK	Bds
3822	–		3364	N			
745			472				
754			3346				
3713	☒		3810			●	
3689			3776				
351			356			●	
3806			611				
718			451				
210			00123				○
775			05555				●
966	◎		*MA078807	☐			
993			*DC105607				

*Overdyed floss used

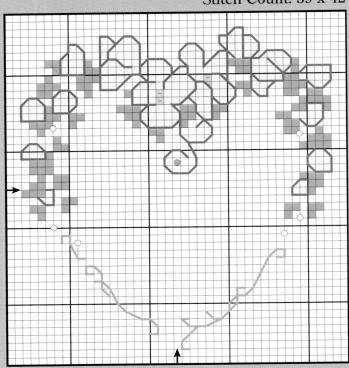

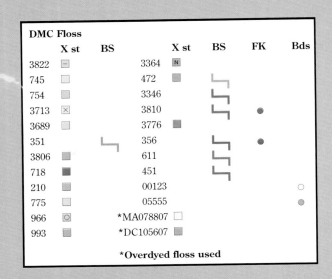

To Rejoice

Code for pages 80-81.

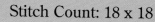

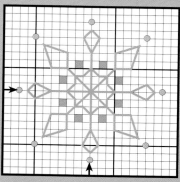

Stitch Count: 18 x 18

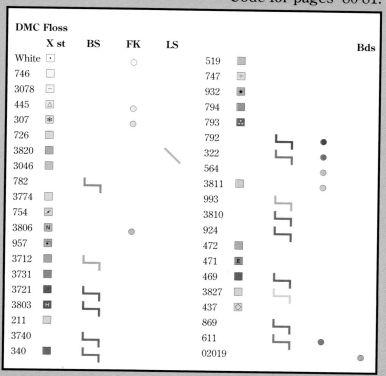

DMC Floss							Bds
	X st	BS	FK	LS			
White	·		○		519	■	
746	☐				747	+	
3078	−				932	★	
445	△		○		794	■	
307	✳		○		793	▨	
726	■				792		●
3820	■				322		●
3046	■				564		●
782		⌐			3811	■	●
3774	■				993		
754	◪				3810		
3806	N		○		924		
957	▣				472	■	
3712	■	⌐			471	E	
3731	■				469	■	
3721	■	⌐			3827	■	
3803	H	⌐			437	○	
211	■	⌐			869		
3740		⌐			611		●
340	■	⌐			02019		●

Stitch Count: 11 x 28

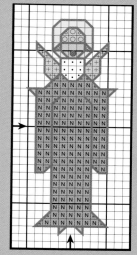

Stitch Count: 23 x 20

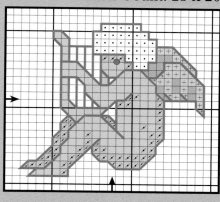

Stitch Count: 16 x 22

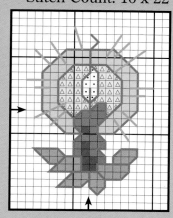

Stitch Count: 37 x 14

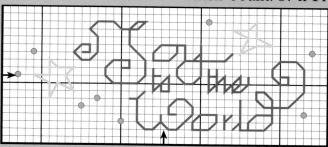

Stitch Count: 18 x 18

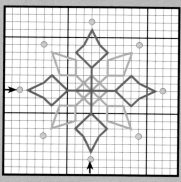

Stitch Count: 51 x 12

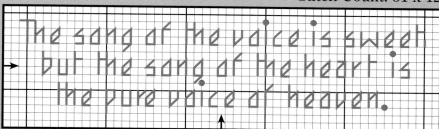

The song of the voice is sweet but the song of the heart is the pure voice of heaven.

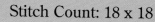

81

Stitch Count: 41 x 38

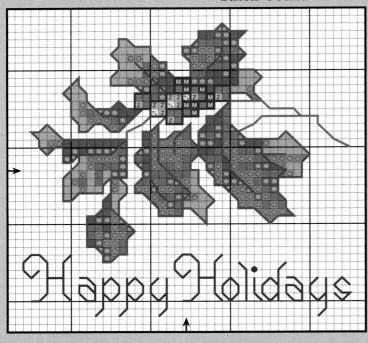

DMC Floss							
	X st	BS	FK		X st	BS	FK
746	▨		○	827	H		
3078	☐			3819	☐		
727	N			3348	☐		
677	✕			3364	U		
676	▨			472	☐		
3046	◎			471	◎		
783		⌐		470	▨		
946		⌐		469	✳		
3770	–			936	▨		
951	☐			935		⌐	
945	▨			3768		⌐	
776	+			437	☐		
899	▨			436	▨		
352	Z			420		⌐	
350	▨			869		⌐	
347	M			648	N		
3328	△			647	▨		
902		⌐	●	646	▨		
828	☐			844		⌐	●

Stitch Count: 48 x 8

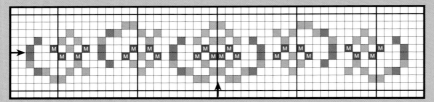

Stitch Count: 18 x 56

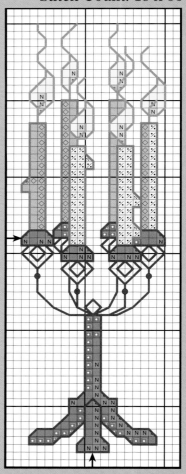

Stitch Count: 51 x 40

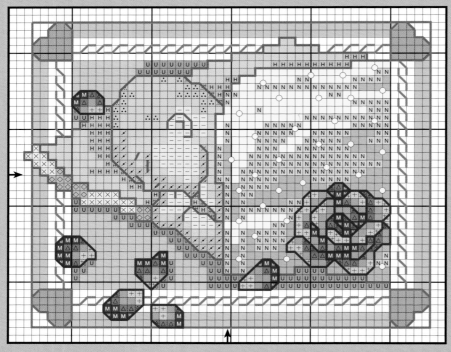

Stitch Count: 54 x 101

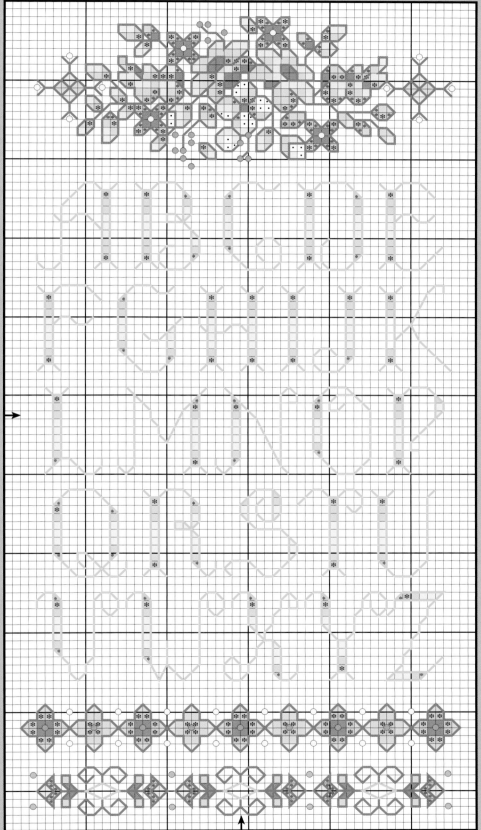

DMC Floss

	X st	BS	Bds
3823			
744			
725			
783			
781			
40123			
42011			
02011			

Stitch Count: 12 x 80

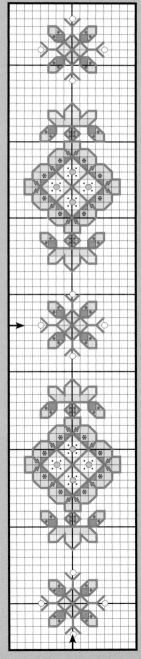

Stitch Count: 14 x 21

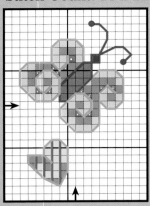

Stitch Count: 40 x 40

Stitch Count: 19 x 15

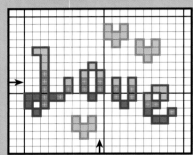

Stitch Count: 10 x 18

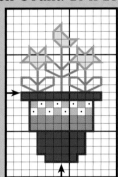

Stitch Count: 34 x 38

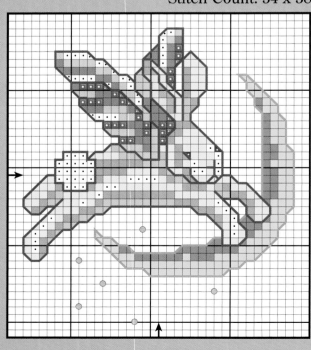

Code for Pages 84-85

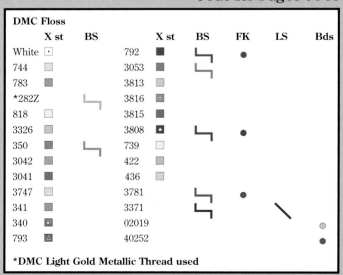

DMC Floss

	X st	BS		X st	BS	FK	LS	Bds
White	·		792		⌐	●		
744			3053		⌐			
783			3813					
*282Z		⌐	3816					
818			3815					
3326			3808	✦	⌐	●		
350		⌐	739		⌐			
3042			422					
3041			436					
3747			3781		⌐	●	\	
341			3371		⌐	●		
340			02019					●
793	△		40252					●

*DMC Light Gold Metallic Thread used

Stitch Count: 49 x 33

Stitch Count: 18 x 31

Stitch Count: 21 x 8

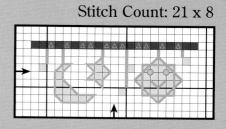

Stitch Count: 18 x 15

Twinkle twinkle little star...

Stitch Count: 43 x 52

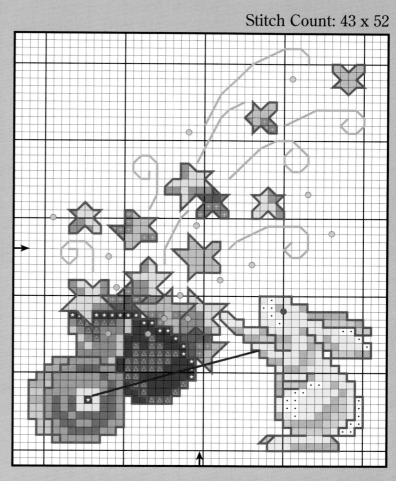

Stitch Count: 24 x 27

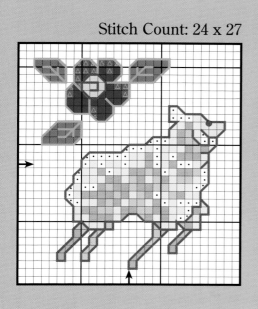

Stitch Count: 129 x 96

Stitch Count: 8 x 74

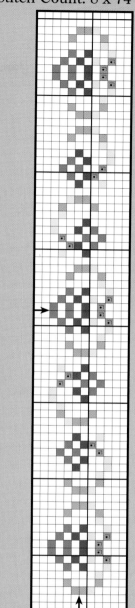

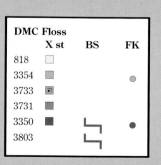

DMC Floss			
	X st	**BS**	**FK**
818			
3354			●
3733			
3731			
3350			●
3803			

Stitch Count: 49 x 29

Stitch Count: 22 x 8

Stitch Count: 62 x 50

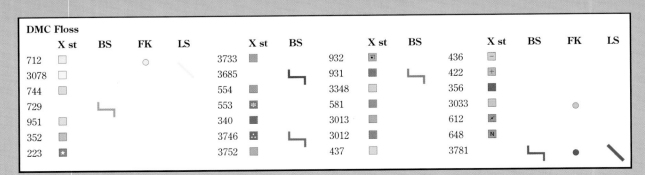

DMC Floss

	X st	BS	FK	LS		X st	BS		X st	BS		X st	BS	FK	LS
712			○		3733				932			436			
3078					3685		⌐		931		⌐	422			
744					554				3348			356			
729		⌐			553				581			3033		○	
951					340				3013			612			
352					3746		⌐		3012			648	N		
223					3752				437			3781		⌐	●	╲

The music of life
is different to each of us...
but, how beautiful the dance!

Continued from page 89.

Stitch Count: 78 x 176

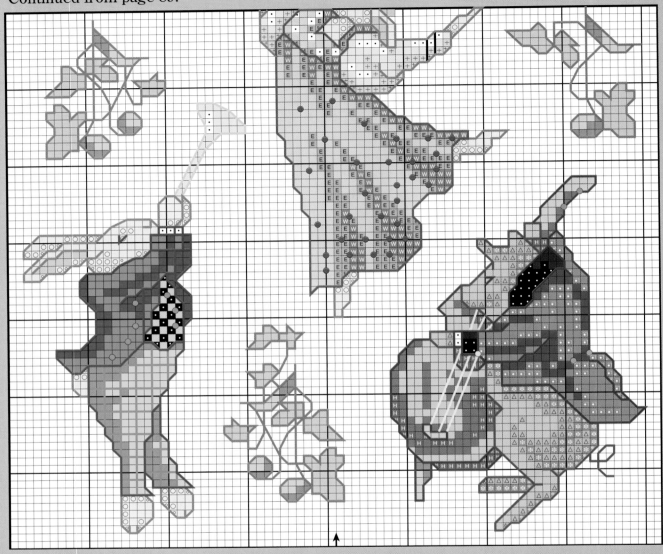

Bottom Left

DMC Floss									
	X st	BS	FK	LS	X st	BS	FK	X st	BS
White	·				347	★		975	H
712			○		817			632	
745					3685		⌐	3031	
743	+				747		⌐	413	
725					519	E		310	
783			●		518	W		*MA023831	
758	△				813			*DC105607	
3778	✳				826	·▫			
761		⌐			824		⌐	*Waterlillies floss used	
963					3051		⌐	●	
3708	✳		●		739	○			
3706			●		436		⌐		
350		⌐			435		⌐		

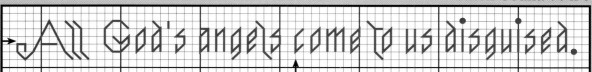

Stitch Count: 38 x 37

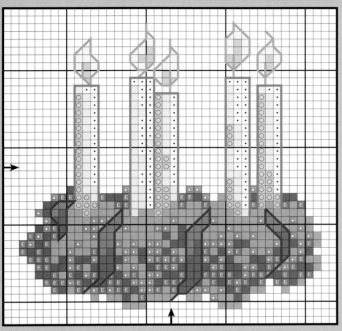

DMC Floss

	X st	BS	FK		X st	BS
White	·			472		
3078				471		
725				3051	E	
677	×			3346		
676	+			3813		
729				502	★	
3046				739		
3045				738	○	
3801				437		
666				420		
815			●	642		
341				640		
340				647		
772				451		
522	N			839		
3053				838		

Stitch Count: 22 x 53

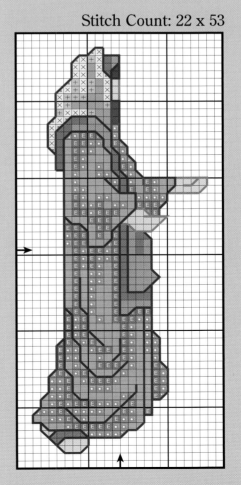

Stitch Count: 38 x 49

91

To Nurture

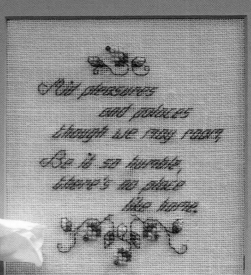

All pleasures
and palaces
though we may roam,
Be it so humble,
there's no place
like home.

Make a memory
with your children,
Spend some time
to show you care.
Toys and trinkets
can't replace those
Precious moments
that you share.

Stitch Count: 20 x 10

Stitch Count: 23 x 27

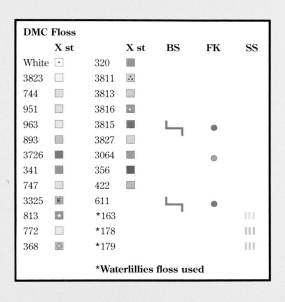

Stitch Count: 36 x 46

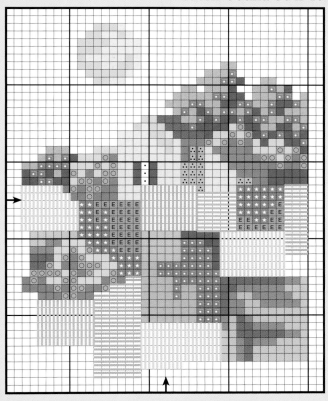

DMC Floss

	X st		X st	BS	FK	SS
White	·	320				
3823		3811				
744		3813				
951		3816				
963		3815			●	
893		3827				
3726		3064				
341		356			●	
747		422				
3325	E	611			●	
813	✦	*163				‖‖
772		*178				‖‖
368	○	*179				‖‖

***Waterlillies floss used**

Stitch Count: 55 x 30

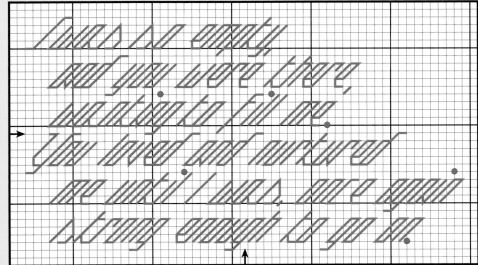

Stitch Count: 15 x 25

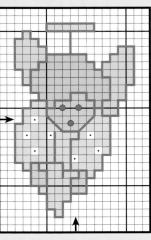

Stitch Count: 43 x 53

Stitch Count: 19 x 12

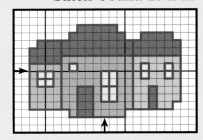

Stitch Count: 29 x 20

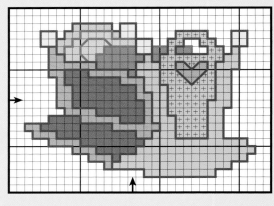

Stitch Count: 16 x 39

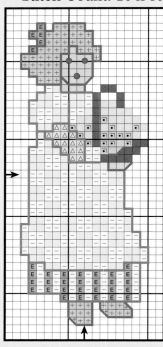

Stitch Count: 25 x 30

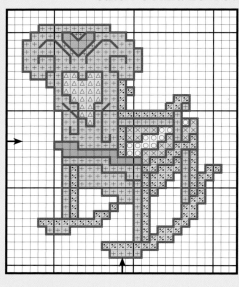

DMC Floss				
	X st	**BS**	**FK**	**Bds**
Ecru	−			
3823	☐			
3078	⊙			
445	☐			
951	☐			
3824	☐			
3706	E			
963	△			
3806	☐			
3722	☐			
341	☐			
828	☐			
747	☒			
3766	☐			
966	·			
772	☐			
368	✳			
502	☐	⌐	●	
3827	☐			
437	⁒			
436	+			
422	☐			
420	☐	⌐		
611	☐	⌐	●	
840	☐	⌐		
839		⌐		
00431				●

Stitch Count: 33 x 47

Stitch Count: 22 x 38

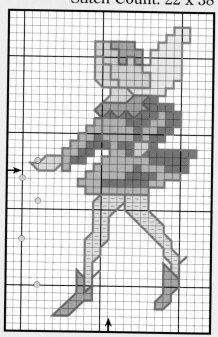

Stitch Count: 44 x 57

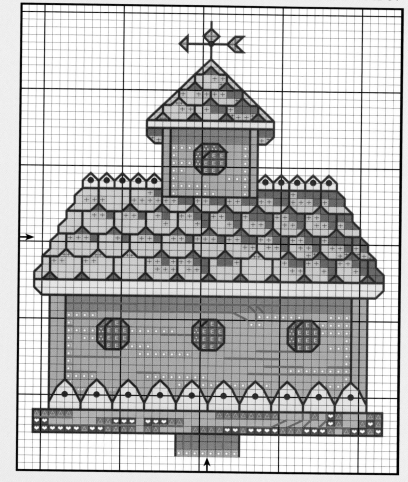

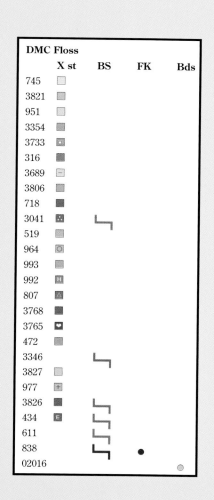

DMC Floss				
	X st	BS	FK	Bds
745				
3821				
951				
3354				
3733				
316				
3689	−			
3806				
718				
3041		⌐		
519				
964	○			
993				
992	H			
807	△			
3768				
3765	♥			
472		⌐		
3346		⌐		
3827				
977	+			
3826		⌐		
434	E	⌐		
611		⌐		
838		⌐	●	
02016				○

Stitch Count: 22 x 33

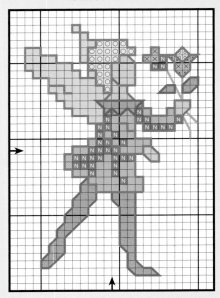

Stitch Count: 44 x 54

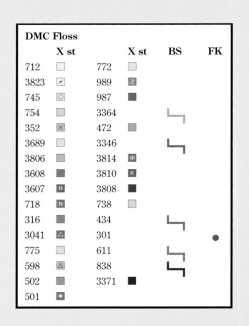

Stitch Count: 32 x 61

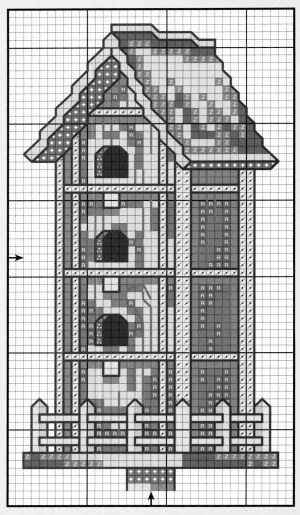

DMC Floss						
	X st		X st		BS	FK
712	☐	772	☐			
3823	◹	989	Z			
745	◯	987	◼			
754	☐	3364		⌐		
352	✕	472	☐			
3689	☐	3346		⌐		
3806	☐	3814	✳			
3608	◼	3810	K			
3607	R	3808	◼			
718	N	738	☐			
316	▨	434		⌐		
3041	▦	301			●	
775	☐	611		⌐		
598	△	838		⌐		
502	☐	3371	◼			
501	✦					

Stitch Count: 56 x 16

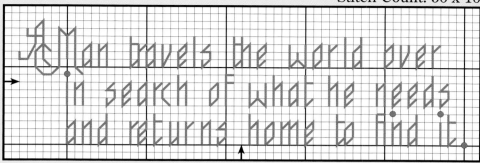

A Man travels the world over in search of what he needs and returns home to find it.

Stitch Count: 36 x 49

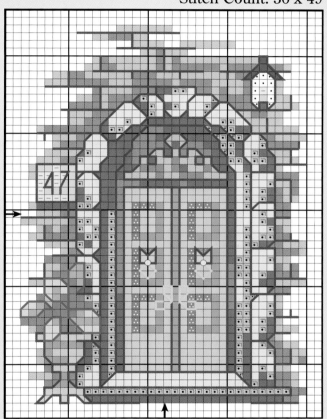

DMC Floss

	X st	BS	FK		X st	BS	FK
White	·			320	■		
3823	−			3364	■		
727	+			472	◉		
744	■	⌐		3051	■	⌐	
945	■			966	■		
352	■			3816	■		
223	★	⌐		3815	■	⌐	
3722	■	⌐	●	739	■		○
3726	■	⌐		437	⊡		
3740	■	⌐		436	E		
341	■			3827	■		
828	■			3064	■		
3325	■			435	■		
813	⠿			611	■	⌐	●
772	■			839	■		
368	■			3781		⌐	

Stitch Count: 22 x 25

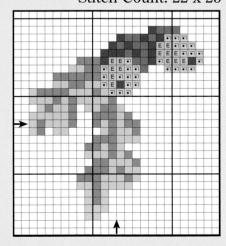

Stitch Count: 32 x 34

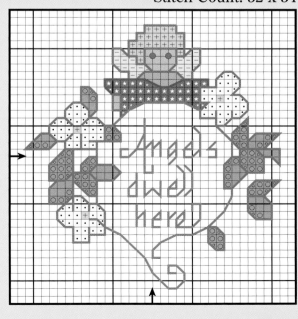

Angels dwell here

97

Stitch Count: 20 x 15

Stitch Count: 27 x 9

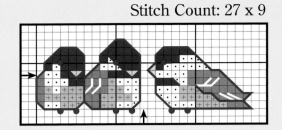

Stitch Count: 18 x 9

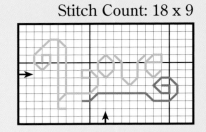

Stitch Count: 26 x 29

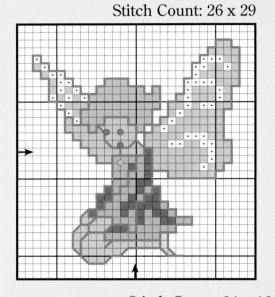

Stitch Count: 29 x 21

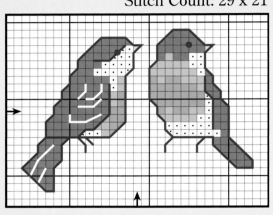

Stitch Count: 19 x 13

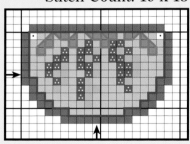

Stitch Count: 24 x 16

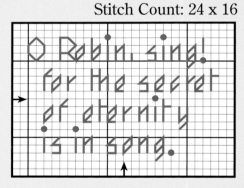

Stitch Count: 57 x 26

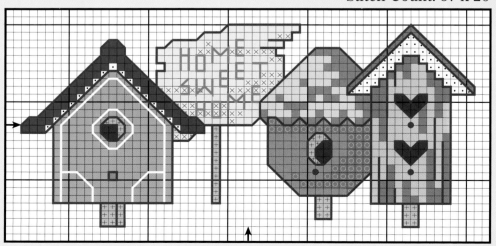

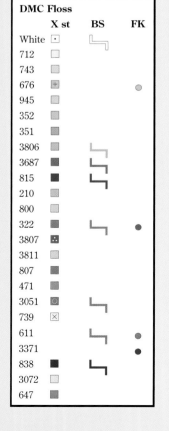

DMC Floss			
	X st	BS	FK
White	·		
712			
743			
676	+		●
945			
352			
351			
3806			
3687			
815			
210			
800			
322			●
3807			
3811			
807			
471			
3051	◉		
739	×		
611			●
3371			●
838			
3072			
647			

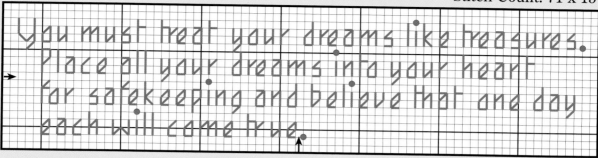

Stitch Count: 41 x 29

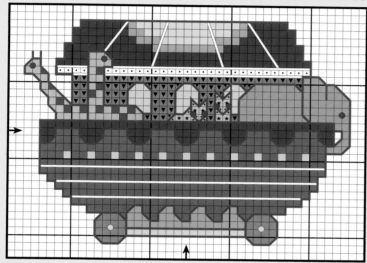

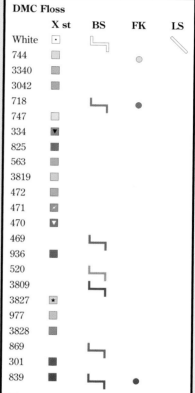

DMC Floss				
	X st	**BS**	**FK**	**LS**
White	·	⌐		/
744			●	
3340				
3042				
718		⌐	●	
747				
334	▼			
825				
563				
3819				
472				
471	◢			
470	▼			
469		⌐		
936		⌐		
520		⌐		
3809		⌐		
3827	★	⌐		
977				
3828				
869		⌐		
301		⌐		
839		⌐	●	

Stitch Count: 48 x 34

Stitch Count: 54 x 7

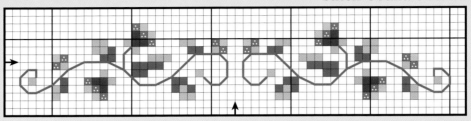

Stitch Count: 54 x 10

Stitch Count: 33 x 69

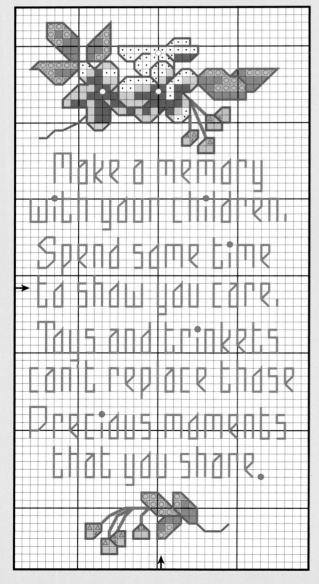

DMC Floss								
	X st	**BS**	**FK**		**X st**	**BS**	**FK**	**LS**
White	·			340	■			
Ecru	–		○	3761			○	
745	▨			828	▨			
761	▨			966	⊠			
760	△			368	▨			
3328	▨			367	■	⌐		
347		⌐	●	993	N			
223		⌐	●	3813	◎			
211	▨			3816	▨			
209	▨			3815			⌐	
208	■			924			⌐	
3747	▨			420				╱
3740	■	⌐		869		⌐		

Stitch Count: 32 x 32

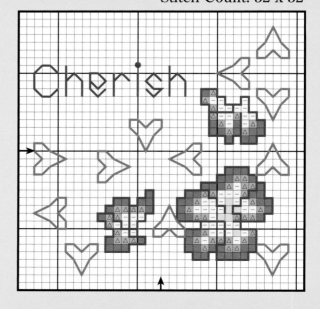

Stitch Count: 19 x 14

DMC Floss

	X st		X st	BS	FK		X st	BS
White	·	224	▦			501	▦	
3823	▼	223		⌐		500		⌐
3822		3722	⬚			437	▦	
951		718		⌐		436	✳	
945	A	3807		⌐	●	422	✦	
3773	▦	503	N			869		⌐
225								

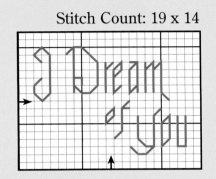

Stitch Count: 42 x 51

Stitch Count: 29 x 51

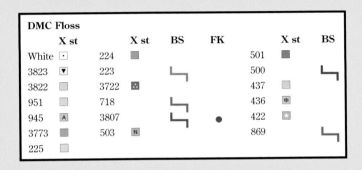

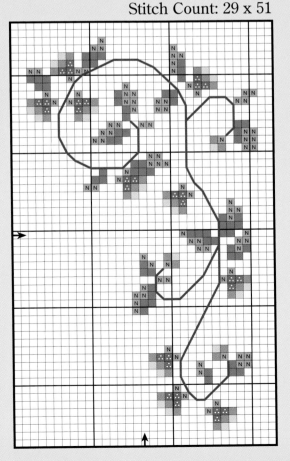

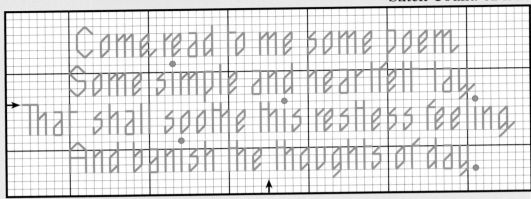

DMC Floss

	X st	BS	FK		X st	BS	FK
White	·			3747			
3823	▼			340			
3822			○	598			
3821		⌐	○	597		⌐	●
951				3811			
945	A			3813	H		
3773				3816			
761				320			
760	✁			924		⌐	
225	⁒			437			
224	✕			436	✳		
223		⌐	●	422	★		
3716				3828			
335				420	+	⌐	
210				869		⌐	
553							

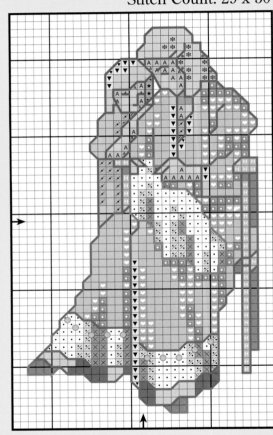

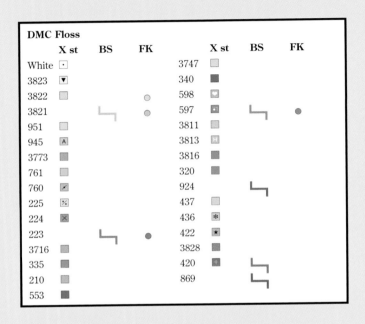

Stitch Count: 31 x 32

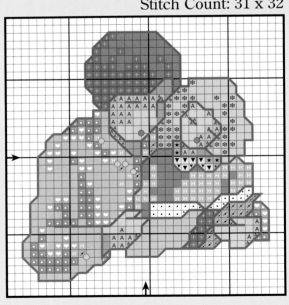

Stitch Count: 24 x 19

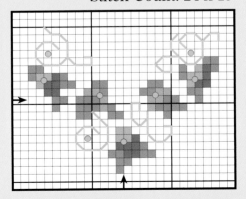

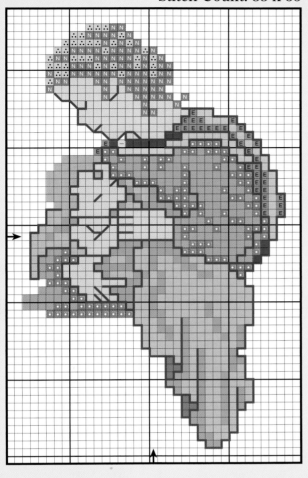

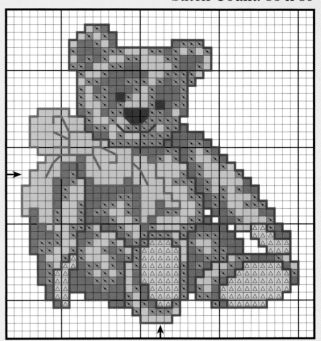

DMC Floss

	X st	BS		X st	BS
White	·		930		
745			3750		⌐
744	−		3364		
676			3362		
729			504		
3829			502	E	
754			500		
3688			436		
3803		⌐	435	N	
3727			3827	△	
3726	⊡		977		
3743			976		
3042	+		3826		
3740			422		
3756			613		
3752	⊙		611	H	
932			801		
931	✳		838	★	⌐

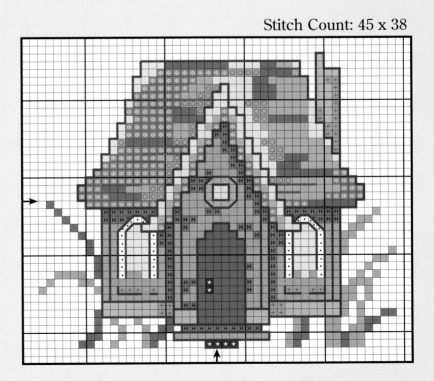

103

To Share

Add some tender loving care to your soft GARDEN
LOVE grows HERE

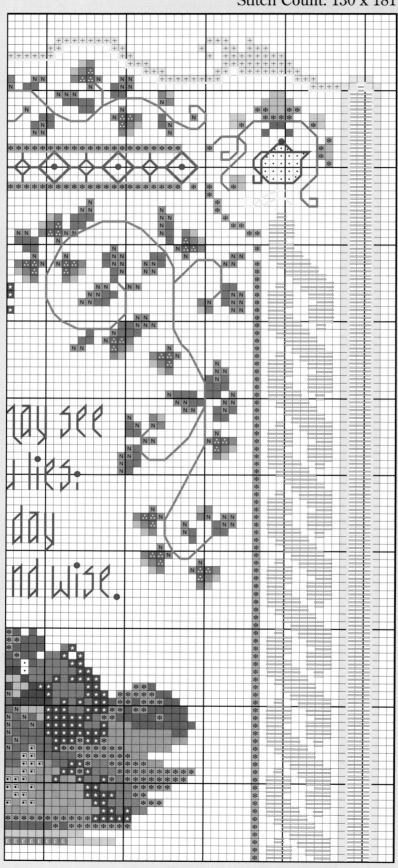

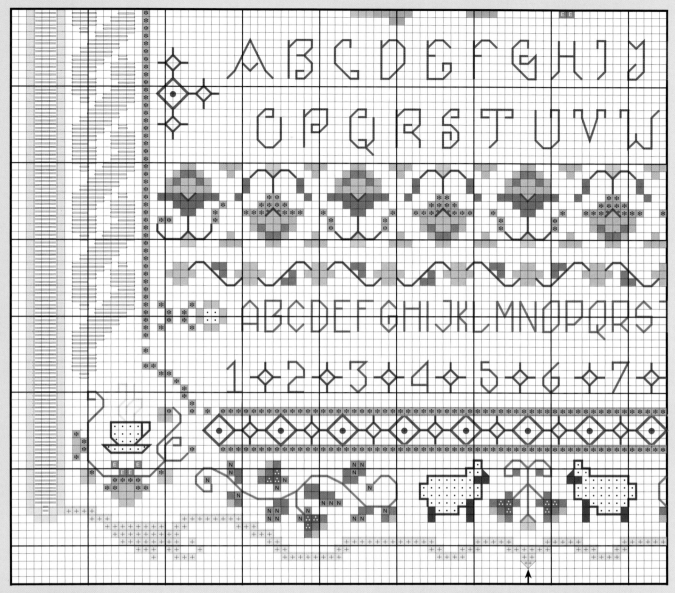

Bottom Left

Code for Pages 105-108

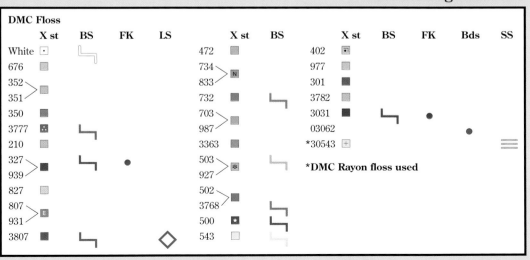

DMC Floss

	X st	BS	FK	LS		X st	BS		X st	BS	FK	Bds	SS
White	·				472			402	⊡				
676					734	N		977					
352 } 351					833			301					
350					732			3782					
3777	⁙				703 } 987			3031			●		
210					3363			03062			●		
327 } 939			●		503 } 927	✳		*30543	⊞			☰	
827					502 } 3768			*DMC Rayon floss used					
807 } 931	E				500	★							
3807				◇	543								

Stitch Count: 14 x 24

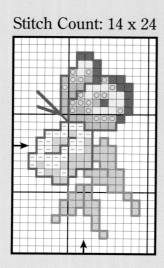

Code for graph at left and page 109.

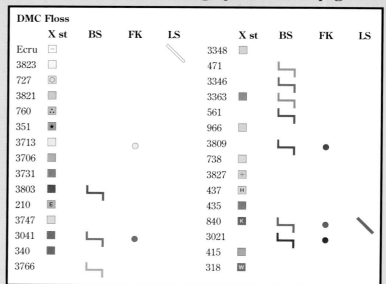

DMC Floss	X st	BS	FK	LS		X st	BS	FK	LS
Ecru	−			/	3348				
3823					471				
727	◎				3346				
3821					3363				
760	∴				561				
351	★				966				
3713			○		3809			●	
3706					738				
3731					3827	+			
3803					437	H			
210	E				435				
3747					840	K		●	/
3041			●		3021			●	
340					415				
3766					318	W			

Stitch Count: 19 x 16

Stitch Count: 10 x 8

Stitch Count: 13 x 14

Stitch Count: 53 x 10

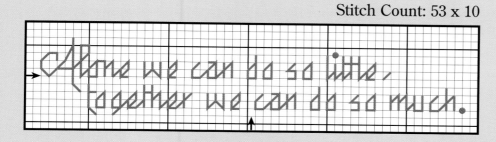

Stitch Count: 18 x 18

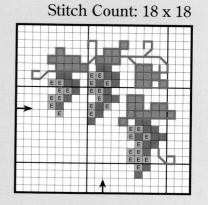

Stitch Count: 52 x 29

Stitch Count: 8 x 20

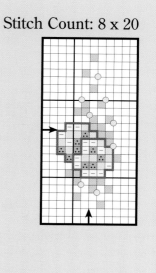

Stitch Count: 46 x 16

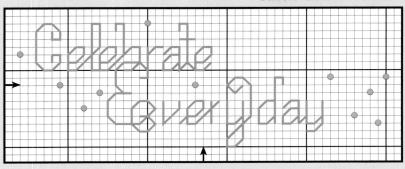

Stitch Count: 21 x 17

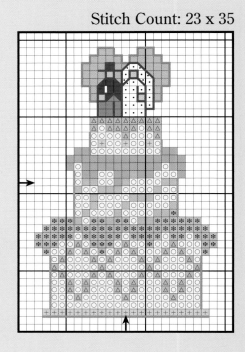

Stitch Count: 23 x 35

DMC Floss

	X st	BS	FK		X st	BS		X st	BS	Bds
White	·	⌐	○	3716	N		334	■		
712	−		○	351	■		311		⌐	
746	⊠			3328		⌐	3348	▨		
745	▢			210	⋰		3012	✴		
3078	◎			3041		⌐	471	▨		
445	▢			3756	▢		3051		⌐	
725	▨			827	▼		936		⌐	
3045		⌐		964	✳		3827	+	⌐	
783	■			3766	▨		869		⌐	
945	▨			3755	◪		844	■	⌐	
760	▨			518		⌐	02019			●
894	△									

Stitch Count: 43 x 49

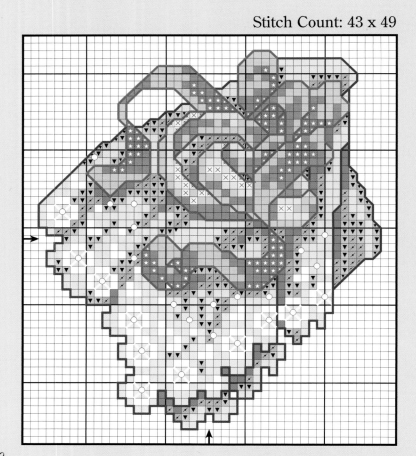

Stitch Count: 22 x 35

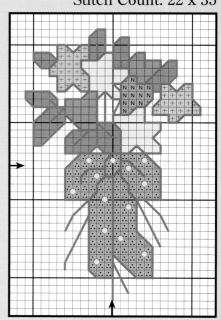

Stitch Count: 25 x 52

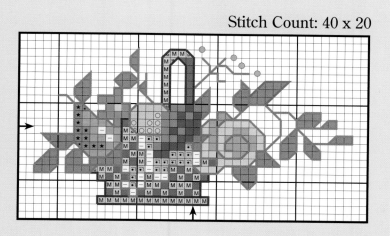

Stitch Count: 13 x 21

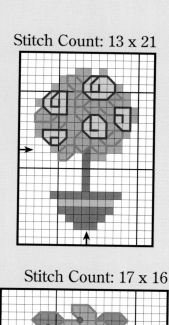

Stitch Count: 17 x 16

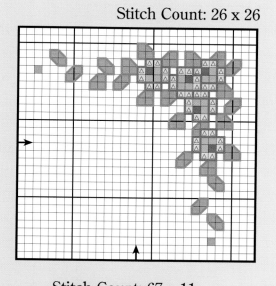

DMC Floss				
	X st	**BS**	**FK**	**Bds**
Ecru	⊟			
3822	▨			
3820	▨		●	
945	▨			
3824	⊡			
963	△			
760	▨			
3722	▣	⌐		
351	▨			
349	▨			
3731	▨			
62013				●
3803	▨	⌐	●	
3756	▨			
799	▨			
472	▨			
471	★			
3051	▨	⌐		
3364	▨			
3363	▨	⌐		
3827	◎			
436	M			
434	▨			
611		⌐		
3021		⌐	●	

Stitch Count: 40 x 20

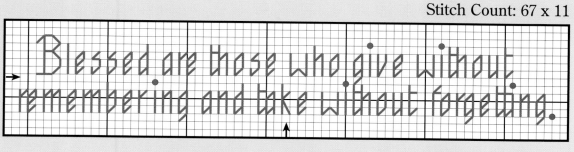

Stitch Count: 26 x 26

Stitch Count: 67 x 11

Blessed are those who give without remembering and take without forgetting.

Stitch Count: 38 x 35

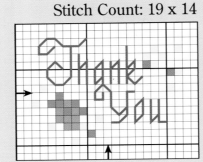

Stitch Count: 19 x 14

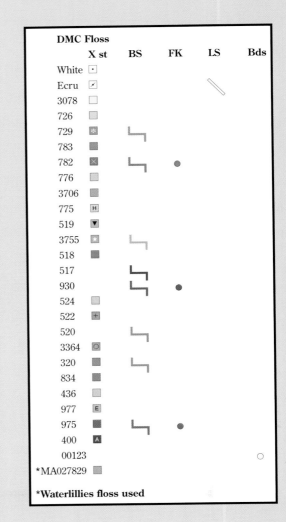

DMC Floss					
	X st	BS	FK	LS	Bds
White	·				
Ecru	◢			/	
3078	▢				
726	▢				
729	✳	⌐			
783	▢				
782	✕	⌐	●		
776	▢				
3706	▢				
775	H				
519	▼				
3755	✷	⌐			
518	▣				
517		⌐			
930		⌐	●		
524	▢				
522	+				
520		⌐			
3364	◎				
320	▢	⌐			
834	▢				
436	▢				
977	E				
975	▢	⌐	●		
400	▣				
00123					○
*MA027829	▢				
*Waterlillies floss used					

Stitch Count: 79 x 40

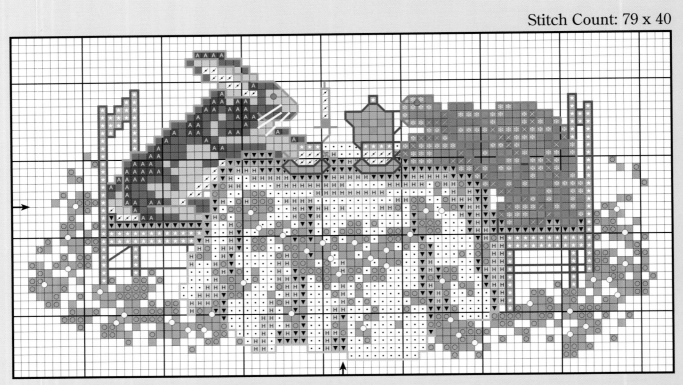

Stitch Count: 35 x 34

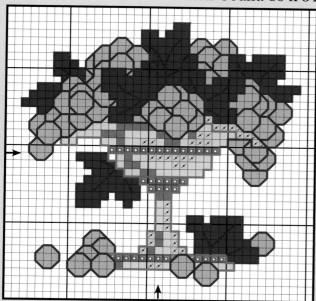

Stitch Count: 21 x 24

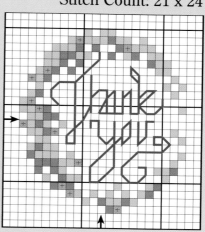

Stitch Count: 74 x 10

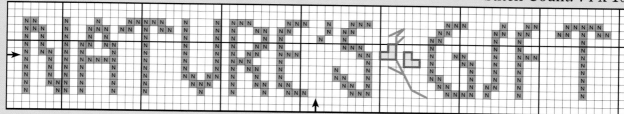

Stitch Count: 34 x 40

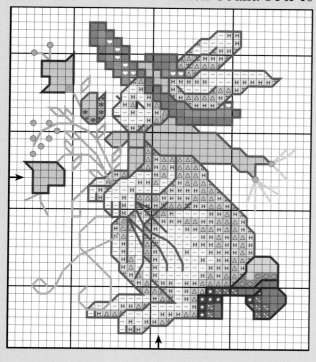

DMC Floss							
	X st	**BS**	**FK**		**X st**	**BS**	**FK**
Ecru	–			3816			
745	H			319			
3822				834			
3821	*			738			
729				437			
783				3827	△		
780		⌐		976			
3713				975			
3354	+			400	*		
3687		⌐		435			
747				434			
3766	⊙	⌐		3829		⌐	●
3807		⌐		801		⌐	
939		⌐		*MA053901			
471		⌐		*MA0061030			
890		⌐		*MA027829			
966				*DC105607	N	⌐	●

***Waterlillies floss used**

Stitch Count: 46 x 26

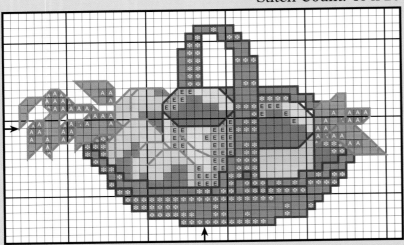

Stitch Count: 50 x 61

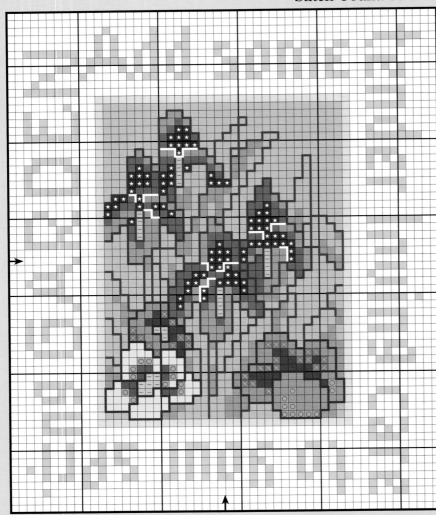

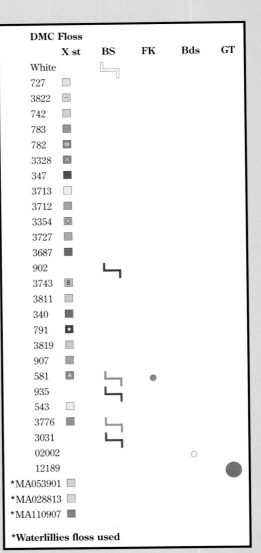

DMC Floss	X st	BS	FK	Bds	GT
White		⌐			
727	□				
3822	–				
742	□				
783	□				
782	✳				
3328	✕				
347	■				
3713	□				
3712	□				
3354	◎				
3727	□				
3687	■				
902		⌐			
3743	E				
3811	□				
340	■				
791	★				
3819	□				
907	□				
581	A	⌐	●		
935		⌐			
543	□				
3776	■	⌐			
3031		⌐			
02002				○	
12189					●
*MA053901	□				
*MA028813	□				
*MA110907	■				

*Waterlillies floss used

Stitch Count: 23 x 31

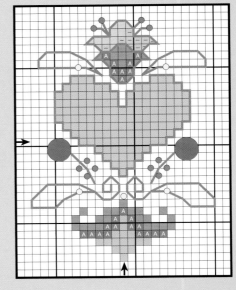

Stitch Count: 29 x 29

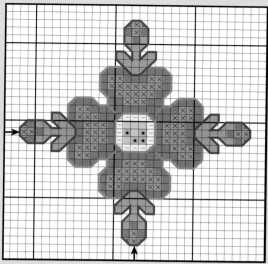

Stitch Count: 29 x 29

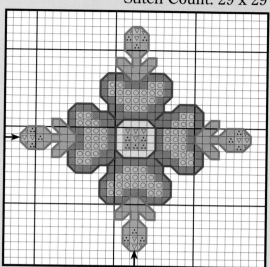

Stitch Count: 50 x 51

DMC Floss		
	X st	BS
Ecru	−	
745		
761		
760	★	
3712	⊠	
3328	⊡	
347	■	
778	⊙	
316		
315		
3743		
3041		
3753	▽	
932	⊞	
928		
926		
503		
501		
472		
581	✳	
935		

To Sow

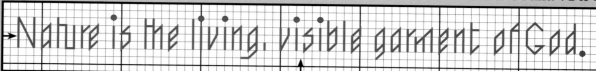

Stitch Count: 39 x 47

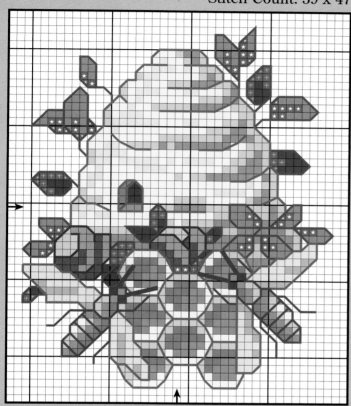

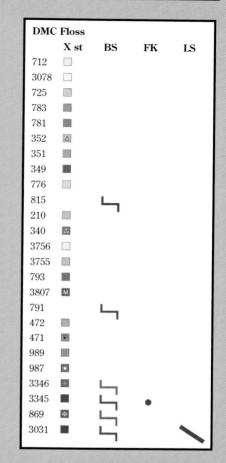

DMC Floss

	X st	BS	FK	LS
712				
3078				
725				
783				
781				
352	△			
351				
349				
776				
815		⌐		
210				
340	⊡			
3756				
3755				
793				
3807	M			
791		⌐		
472				
471	⊡			
989				
987	✷			
3346	+	⌐		
3345		⌐	●	
869	✳	⌐		
3031		⌐		╱

Stitch Count: 77 x 9

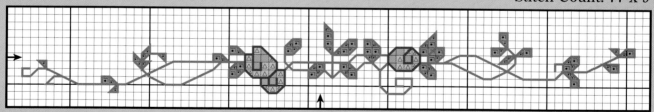

Stitch Count: 25 x 12

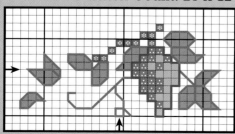

Stitch Count: 5 x 15

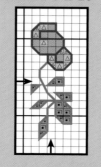

Stitch Count: 24 x 17

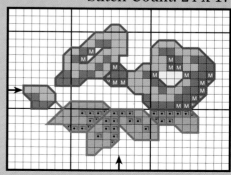

Stitch Count: 11 x 16

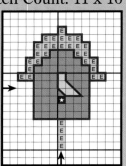

Stitch Count: 17 x 18

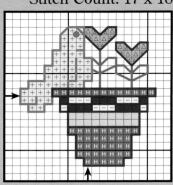

Stitch Count: 33 x 60

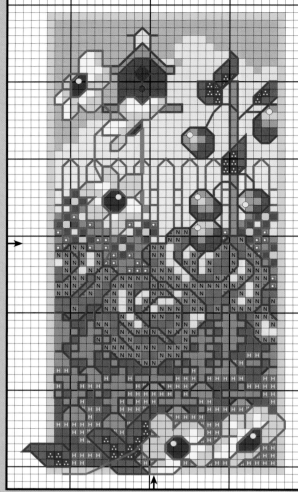

Stitch Count: 30 x 8

Stitch Count: 30 x 18

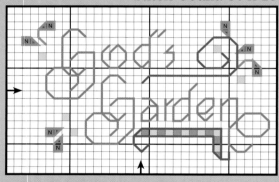

Stitch Count: 15 x 10

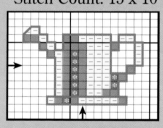

Stitch Count: 13 x 11

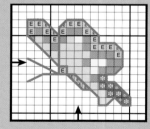

Stitch Count: 9 x 16

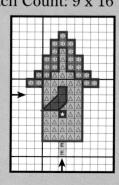

Stitch Count: 16 x 20

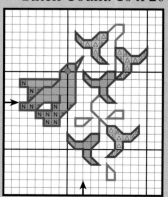

DMC Floss							
	X st	BS	FK		X st	BS	FK
Ecru	⊟			3807	■	⌐	
712	☐		○	472	▨	⌐	
3823	⊞			471	N	⌐	
3078	☐			470	■		
727	☐			989	■		
725	▨			987	▨		
783	▨			3346	■	⌐	
781		⌐		3345	▨	⌐	
776	☐			500	■	⌐	
760	△			436	E		
351	▨			420	H		
349	■			869	■	⌐	
221	■	⌐		612	▨		
341	▨			611	✳	⌐	●
3756	☐			3031	■	⌐	●
3755	▨			3021	★	⌐	

Stitch Count: 60 x 9

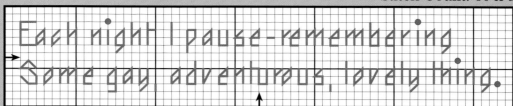

Each night I pause-remembering
Some gay, adventurous, lovely thing.

Stitch Count: 41 x 51

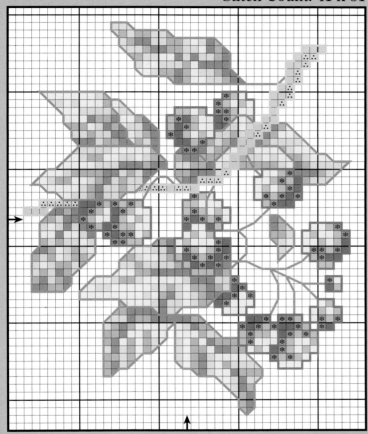

Stitch Count: 14 x 9

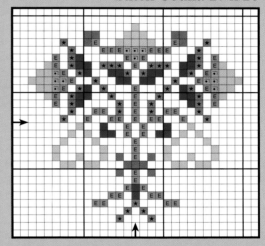

Stitch Count: 27 x 26

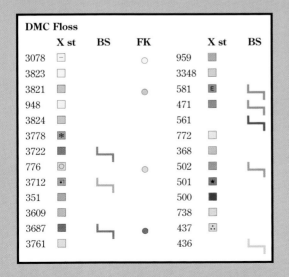

Stitch Count: 35 x 27

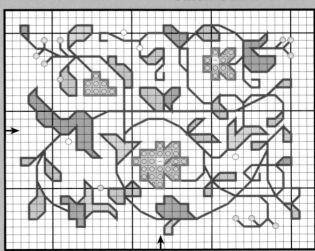

DMC Floss

	X st	BS	FK		X st	BS
3078	⊟			959	■	
3823	☐			3348	☐	
3821	■		○	581	E	⌐
948	☐			471	■	⌐
3824	■			561		⌐
3778	✱			772	☐	
3722	■	⌐		368	■	
776	◎		●	502	■	⌐
3712	▪	⌐		501	★	
351	■	⌐		500	■	
3609	☐			738	☐	
3687	■	⌐	●	437	▣	
3761	☐			436		⌐

119

Stitch Count: 24 x 19

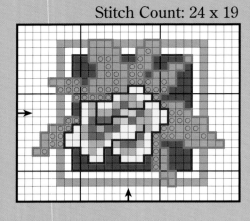

Stitch Count: 18 x 18

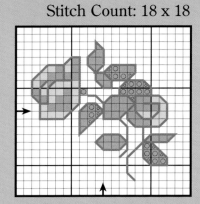

Stitch Count: 21 x 24

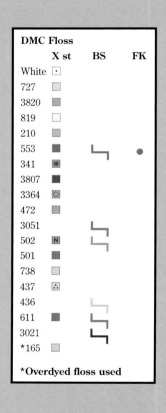

Stitch Count: 44 x 54

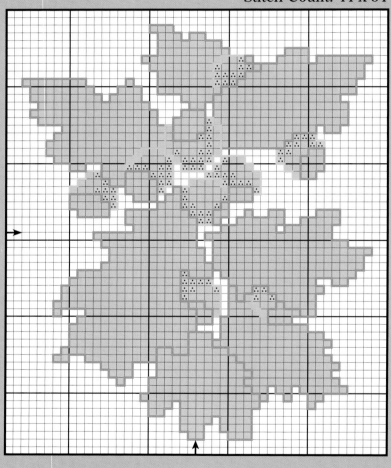

DMC Floss

	X st	BS	FK
White	⋅		
727			
3820			
819			
210			
553		⌐	●
341	✳		
3807			
3364	◎		
472			
3051		⌐	
502	N	⌐	
501			
738			
437	⋅⋅		
436		⌐	
611		⌐	
3021		⌐	
*165			

*Overdyed floss used

Stitch Count: 26 x 26

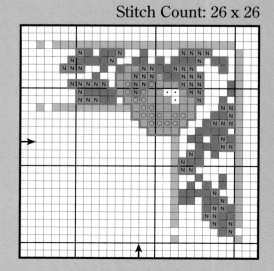

Stitch Count: 46 x 18

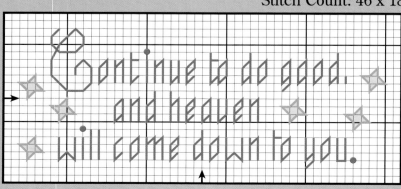

Stitch Count: 65 x 11

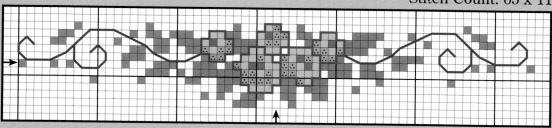

Stitch Count: 38 x 58

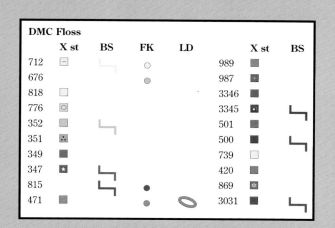

Stitch Count: 30 x 29

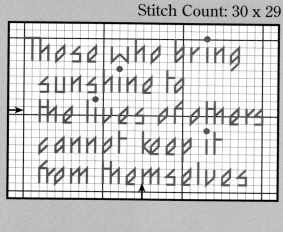

Those who bring
sunshine to
the lives of others
cannot keep it
from themselves

Stitch Count: 23 x 27

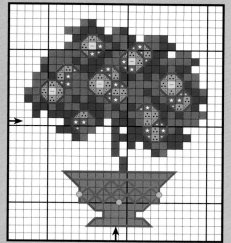

DMC Floss							
	X st	**BS**	**FK**	**LD**		**X st**	**BS**
712	−		○		989		
676			○		987	+	
818					3346		
776	○				3345		└
352		└			501		
351					500		└
349					739		
347	★	└			420		
815		└	●		869		
471		└	●	○	3031		└

Stitch Count: 12 x 15

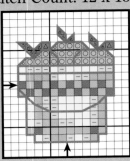

Stitch Count: 23 x 22

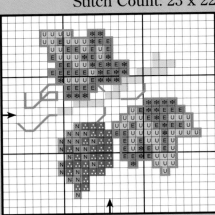

Stitch Count: 16 x 31

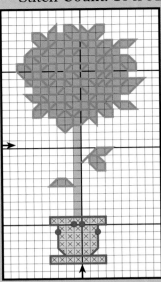

Stitch Count: 26 x 12

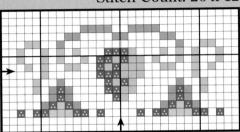

Stitch Count: 29 x 5

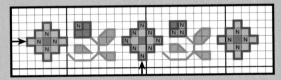

Stitch Count: 40 x 48

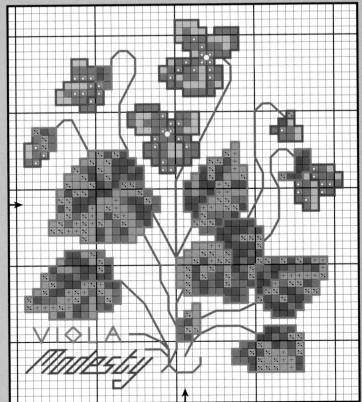

DMC Floss							
	X st	BS	FK		X st	BS	FK
Ecru			○	3348	U		
3078				472			
744	−			471	△		
3821				3819			
352	◎			581	E		
3609				523	+		
210				522			
3041		⌐		503	⅍		
333		⌐		501			⌐
800				367			⌐
341	N			991			⌐
340				3808			⌐
3746	⊞			437			
3807	⊡			3827	✕		
3750				422			
3364		⌐		611			⌐
3363	✳	⌐		839			●

Stitch Count: 49 x 30

Stitch Count: 36 x 31

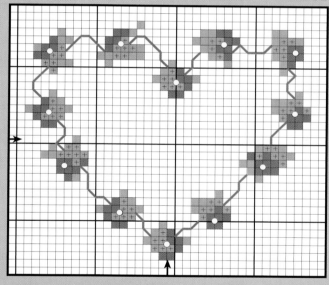

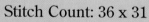

Stitch Count: 70 x 21

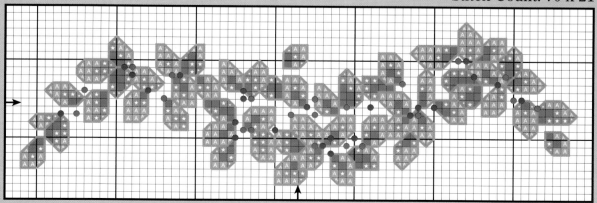

DMC Floss				
	X st	BS	LS	Bds
3822	–			
951				
3712				
3743				
3042	+			
3041				
552				
775				
930		⌐	/	
3819				
581		⌐		
3051		⌐		
3053				
472	A			
471	⊞			
470				
520		⌐		
3364				
3362		⌐		
502	◎	⌐		
422				
402				
3790				
3031		⌐		
40161				○
42024				●
00157				●
02025				●

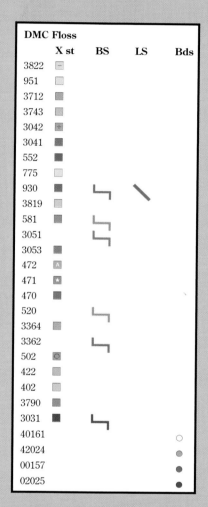

Stitch Count: 44 x 24

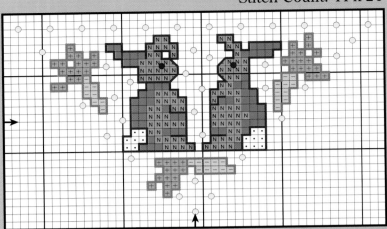

Stitch Count: 11 x 13

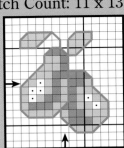

Stitch Count: 22 x 14

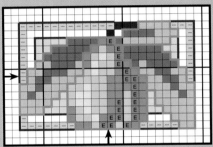

Stitch Count: 46 x 20

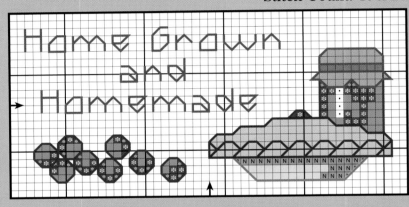

Stitch Count: 38 x 46

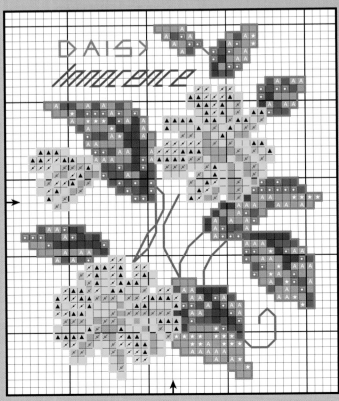

DMC Floss

	X st	BS	FK		X st	BS	FK
White				523			
712				522			
445			○	3363	E	⌐	
727				367			
444				503	A		
3822	▲			501		⌐	
3821				3817			
3820				3815			
3354				991		⌐	
3731				3808		⌐	
3350		⌐		738			
3761				3827	−		
794				436			
3807				611		⌐	
311		⌐		801		⌐	
3750				3021	■	⌐	
3348				762			
472	+			415	N		
3819				414			
581		⌐		413		⌐	●
3051		⌐					

Stitch Count: 40 x 41

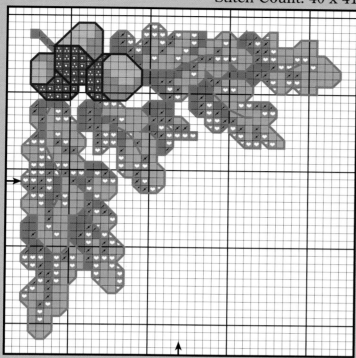

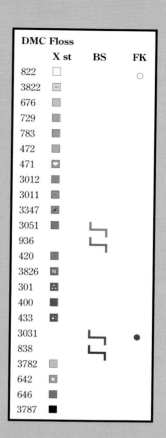

DMC Floss

	X st	BS	FK
822	☐		○
3822	⊟		
676	▦		
729	▩		
783	▩		
472	▨		
471	▨		
3012	▦		
3011	◉		
3347	◪		
3051	▨	⌐	
936			
420	▨		
3826	N		
301	▦		
400	▪		
433	▣		
3031		⌐	●
838			
3782	▨		
642	★		
646	▨		
3787	■		

Stitch Count: 65 x 41

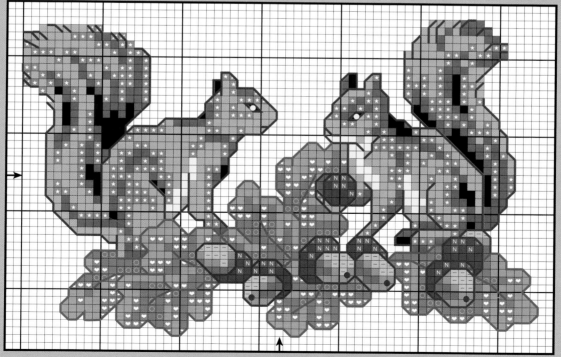

125

DMC = Kreinik		DMC = Kreinik		DMC = Kreinik		DMC = Kreinik	
Snow White	Blanc	367	1835/3425	554	3312	725	2514
Ecru		368	1832/1842	561	146	726	522
Creme/F2/F13		369	1841	562	144	727	2521
208	1334/3335	370	2214	563	143/211	729	
209	1342/3334	372	3833	564	141	2234/2243/2533	
210	3334	400	4141/4215	580	516	730	3724
211	3333	402	632/2622	581	2124	731	516/2214
221	4623/4624	407	4611	597	132	732	2124
223	4622	413	3445	598	1721/1723	733	2212
224	4621	414	3442	602	3014	734	2212
225	1011	415	3441	603	3013	738	3821/4112
300	4142	420	526	604	3012	739	4241
301	2625	422	3812	605	3021	740	624
304	943/1026	433	4116/4122	606	915/935	741	611/624
307	543	434	4516	608	635	742	545
309	2934/2945	435	4236	610	3835	743	536
310	Noir	436	4235	611	4534	744	2532
311	1716	437	4234	612	3833	745	2542
312	1715	444	536	613	3832	746	2541
315	4646	451	3414	632	4143	747	1723
316	4634	452	3413/3414	640	3834	754	1012
317	3445	453	3412/3413	642	3713	758	2912
318	3442	469	2125	644	3422	760	2932/2943
319	1845	470	245/2125	645	3844	761	1013/2931
320	1834	471	2114	646	3843	762	3441
321	941/943	472	2122/2123	647	1734	772	2113
322	4922	498	945/1026	648	3841	775	1441
326	1026	500	1846	666	915/935	776	2941
327	3315	501	1844/3426	676	2242	778	4631/4634
333	1344	503	1843	677	2141	780	3816/3826
334	1434	504	1822	680	524	781	2516/3825
335	3014	517	1446/1725	699	225	782	2244
336	1423	518	1444	700	226	783	2244
340	1343	519	1442	701	235	791	1345
341	1433	520	3726	702	224/236	793	4913
347	2924	522	1832/1842	703	223	794	1434
349	915/935	523	1841	704	221	796	116
350	914/934	524	3423	712	Brut	797	4924
351	924	535	3844	718	1043	798	4923
352	932/933	543	3431	720	634	799	4922
353	921/2913	550	3336/3315	721	645	800	4921
355	2636	552	3314	722	633	801	4115
356	4612	553	3313			806	126

DMC	= Kreinik		DMC	= Kreinik		DMC	= Kreinik		DMC	= Kreinik
807	125		907	244		973	536		3350	3025
809	1434		909	225		975	4215		3354	3021/3011
813	1443		910	226		976	4212		3362	3726
814	2926/4625		911	214		977	611/2546		3363	1832/1833
815	2925		913	213		986	1845		3364	1831/3723
816	946		917	1043		987	2116		3371	4136
817	916		918	4142		988	2115		3609	1312
818	2942		919	2636		989	234		3685	3026
819	1011		920	2625		991	1826		3687	3023/3024
820	116		921	2615		992	5013		3688	1042
822	3711/3811		922	644		993	1823		3689	3031
823	163/1425		924	205		995	114		3705	914/934
824	115		926	1745		996	113		3706	932
825	1446		927	1744		3011	516		3708	1021/1022
826	113		928	1742		3012	2124		3712	2914
827	1442		930	1715		3013	3722		3713	1011
828	1721		931	1714		3021	3846		3716	3021
829	526		932	1712		3022	3715		3726	4645
830	2214		934	3726		3023	3422		3727	3031
831	2214		935	2126		3024	3421/3841		3731	3013
832	2235		936	2136		3031	4115		3733	3012
833	2233		937	516		3032	4534		3743	3322
834	2242		938	4124		3033	3711		3746	1343
838	4124		939	165		3041	4635		3747	4911
839	3433		945	2632		3042	4633		3750	1716
840	3345/3434		946	634		3045	3742		3752	1712
841	3341		948	2911		3046	2231		3755	112
842	3431/4531		950	2912		3047	2541/2542		3760	1445
844	3844/3846		951	4241		3051	2126		3761	1722
869	526		954	143/211		3052	3723		3765	126
890	1836/1845		955	141		3053	3722		3766	125
891	914		956	1024		3064	4611		3768	1745
893	1014		957	1022		3072	111/1813		3770	F13
894	1022		958	5013		3078	2521		3772	4611
895	1845		959	5012		3325	4921		3774	2911
898	4131/4124		961	3013		3326	3021		3776	644
899	2933		962	3022		3328	2915		3778	2642
900	635/636		963	2942		3340	912		3779	2912
902	2926/4626		964	5011		3341	911		3787	3344
904	2116		966	142		3345	2116		3799	3445
905	224		970	634		3346	2115			
906	223		971	633		3347	2114			
			972	544/545		3348	2113			

mm-millimetres cm-centimetres
inches to millimetres and centimetres

inches	mm	cm	inches	cm	inches	cm
⅛	3	0.3	9	22.9	30	76.2
¼	6	0.6	10	25.4	31	78.7
½	13	1.3	12	30.5	33	83.8
⅝	16	1.6	13	33.0	34	86.4
¾	19	1.9	14	35.6	35	88.9
⅞	22	2.2	15	38.1	36	91.4
1	25	2.5	16	40.6	37	94.0
1¼	32	3.2	17	43.2	38	96.5
1½	38	3.8	18	45.7	39	99.1
1¾	44	4.4	19	48.3	40	101.6
2	51	5.1	20	50.8	41	104.1
2½	64	6.4	21	53.3	42	106.7
3	76	7.6	22	55.9	43	109.2
3½	89	8.9	23	58.4	44	111.8
4	102	10.2	24	61.0	45	114.3
4½	114	11.4	25	63.5	46	116.8
5	127	12.7	26	66.0	47	119.4
6	152	15.2	27	68.6	48	121.9
7	178	17.8	28	71.1	49	124.5
8	203	20.3	29	73.7	50	127.0

Index